Encouraged to Pray

–

Classic Sermons on Prayer

Charles Haddon Spurgeon

Encouraged to Pray

© 2017 by Cross-Points Books

CONTENTS

SERIES INTRODUCTION

The Rich Theology Made Accessible Series seeks to bolster the faith of busy Christians by making rich theology from time past more accessible.

Current Titles:
- Volume 1: *The Chief Exercise of Faith: John Calvin on Prayer*
- Volume 2: *Gospel Hope for Anxious Hearts: Trading Fear and Worry for the Peace of God* by Charles Spurgeon
- Volume 3: *Encouraged to Pray: Classic Sermons on Prayer* by Charles Spurgeon
- Volume 4: *Lessons from the Apostle Paul's Prayers* by Charles Spurgeon
- Volume 5: *Our Savior's Cries from the Cross* by Charles Spurgeon

Visit Cross-Points.org/richtheology to learn more or to explore additional titles.

JOIN THE CONVERSATION

Share your thoughts and favorite quotes on social media using the hashtag #EncouragedtoPray or by mentioning us on social media:
- Twitter: @Cross_Points
- Facebook: @CrossPoints.Resources

FOREWORD

If you've ever had a car stuck in the mud (or snow for colder-climate readers), you'll know the frustration. You put the pedal to the metal and don't budge while your wheels spin hopelessly.

Prayer often seems like that. We *desire* to move forward in prayer, but our meager efforts feel like futile wheel-spinning. And we lose heart. In such a case, we need a push from behind and traction for our spinning tires to get going again. Thankfully, God knows our struggles and meets us in Scripture to push us out of the ruts we are in and move forward.

In *Encouraged to Pray*, Charles Spurgeon's faithful expositions of Scripture will provide the push and traction you need to move forward in joyful and effective prayer. Here is a glimpse of four precious jewels Spurgeon mined from the quarry of prayer:

1. **If you struggle getting started in prayer, read the Bible first and respond to what God says.**
"If the flesh in its weakness hampers the spirit, then let the Bible reading come before the praying, that the soul may be awakened thereby."

2. **God, our all-powerful heavenly Father, is able and willing to grant our requests.**
"Do you always remember, beloved, in coming to the mercy-seat, that you are coming to a King, and to One who gives like a King? Do you always open your mouth

wide, and ask great things of the King who is so ready to bestow them upon you?"

3. Our gracious Father doesn't need eloquent prayers to hear the cries of His children.

"A mother can translate baby-talk: she comprehends incomprehensible noises. Even so doth our Father in heaven know all about our poor baby talk, for our prayer is not much better."

4. When we don't feel like praying, pray for help.

"Not to pray because you do not feel fit to pray is like saying, 'I will not take medicine because I am too ill.' Pray for prayer: pray yourself, by the Spirit's assistance, into a praying frame."

Much more can be said about how Spurgeon will encourage you to pray, but I'll just invite you to read this book.

Let me close with one last thing: *Being encouraged* to pray is not the goal of this book. *Praying is. Communion with the Father and Son by the Spirit is. Being released from self-imposed burdens that hinder our prayers is. Making a difference in the world by crying out to our loving God for mercy is.* If you read this book and your prayer life remains the same, you've missed the point.

Grab your Bible, a pen, and your prayer book. Examine your prayer life and actively implement the gospel riches Spurgeon shares. In doing so, you will not only find yourself encouraged to pray, but actually praying.

Kevin Halloran (@kp_halloran)
Series Editor, blogger at Anchored in Christ
Portoviejo, Ecuador
November 2017

1
TRUE PRAYER, TRUE POWER!

"Therefore I say unto you, what things soever ye desire, when ye pray, believe that ye receive them, and ye shall have them."
—*St. Mark 11:24*

"God has promised to hear prayer, and he will perform his promise."

~

THIS verse has something to do with the faith of miracles; but I think it hath far more reference to the miracle of faith. We shall at any rate, this morning, consider it in that light. I believe that this text is the inheritance not only of the apostles, but of all those who walk in the faith of the apostles, believing in the promises of the Lord Jesus Christ. The advice which Christ gave to the twelve and to his immediate followers, is repeated to us in God's Word this morning. May we have grace constantly to obey it. "What things soever ye desire, when ye pray, believe that ye receive them, and ye shall have them." How many persons there are who complain that they do not enjoy prayer. They do not neglect it, for they dare not; but they would neglect it if they dared, so far are they from finding any pleasure therein. And have we not to lament that sometimes the chariot-wheels are taken off, and we drive right heavily when we are in supplication? We spend the time allotted, but we rise from our knees unrefreshed, like a man who has lain upon his bed but has not slept so as to really recover his strength. When the time comes round again conscience drives us to our knees, but there is no sweet fellowship with God. There is no telling out of our wants to him in the firm conviction that he will supply them. After having gone again through a certain round of customary utterances, we rise from our knees perhaps more troubled in conscience and more distressed in mind than we were before. There are many Christians, I think, who have to complain of this—that they pray not so much because it is a blessed thing to be allowed to draw near to God, as because they must pray, because it is their duty, because they feel that if they did not, they would lose one of the sure evidences of their being Christians. Brethren, I do not condemn you; but at the same time, if I may be the means of lifting you up this morning from so low a state of grace into a higher and more healthy atmosphere, my soul shall be exceeding glad. If I can show you a more excellent way; if from this time forth you may come to look at prayer as your element, as one of the most delightful exercises of your life; if you shall come to esteem it more than your necessary food, and to value it as one of heaven's best luxuries, surely I shall have answered a great end, and you shall have to thank God for a great blessing.

Give me then your attention while I beg you, first,

to look at the text; secondly, *to look about you;* and then, *to look above you.*

I. First, LOOK AT THE TEXT. If you look at it carefully, I think you will perceive the essential qualities which are necessary to any great success and prevalence in prayer. According to our Saviour's description of prayer, there should always be some *definite objects* for which we should plead. He speaks of *things*—"what things soever ye desire." It seems then that he did not put it that God's children would go to him to pray when they have nothing to pray for. Another essential qualification of prayer is *earnest desire;* for the Master supposes here that when we pray we have desires. Indeed it is not prayer, it may be something like prayer, the outward form or the bare skeleton, but it is not the living thing, the all-prevailing, almighty thing, called prayer, unless there be a fulness and overflowing of desires. Observe, too, that *faith* is an essential quality of successful prayer—"believe that ye receive them." Ye cannot pray so as to be heard in heaven and answered to your soul's satisfaction, unless you believe that God really hears and will answer you. One other qualification appears here upon the very surface, namely, that *a realizing expectation* should always go with a firm faith—"believe that ye receive them." Not merely believe that "ye shall" but believe that "ye do" receive them—count them as if they were received, reckon them as if you had them already, and act as if you had them—act as if you were sure you should have them—"believe that ye receive them, and ye shall have them." Let us review these four qualities, one by one.

To make prayer of any value, there should be

3

definite objects for which to plead. My brethren, we often ramble in our prayers after this, that, and the other, and we get nothing because in each we do not really desire anything. We chatter about many subjects, but the soul does not concentrate itself upon any one object. Do you not sometimes fall on your knees without thinking beforehand what you mean to ask God for? You do so as a matter of habit, without any motion of your heart. You are like a man who should go to a shop and not know what articles he would procure. He may perhaps make a happy purchase when he is there, but certainly it is not a wise plan to adopt. And so the Christian in prayer may afterwards attain to a real desire, and get his end, but how much better would he speed if having prepared his soul by consideration and self-examination, he came to God for an object at which he was about to aim with a real request. Did we ask an audience at Her Majesty's court, we should be expected to reply to the question, "What do you wish to see her for?" We should not be expected to go into the presence of Royalty, and then to think of some petition after we came there. Even so with the child of God. He should be able to answer the great question, "What is thy petition and what is thy request, and it shall be done unto thee?" Imagine an archer shooting with his bow, and not knowing where the mark is! Would he be likely to have success? Conceive a ship on a voyage of discovery, putting to sea without the captain having any idea of what he was looking for! Would you expect that he would come back heavily laden either with the discoveries of science, or with treasures of gold? In everything else you have a plan. You do not go to work without knowing that there is something that you designed to make; how is it that you go to God without knowing what you design to have? If you had some object you would never find prayer to be a dull and heavy work; I am persuaded that you would long for it. You would say, "I have something that I want. Oh that I could draw near my God, and ask him for it; I have a need, I want to have it satisfied, and I long till I can get alone, that I may pour out my heart before him, and ask him for this great thing after which my soul so earnestly pants." You will find it more helpful to your prayers if you have some objects at which you aim, and I think also if you have some persons whom you will mention. Do not merely plead with God for sinners in general, but always mention some in particular. If you are a Sunday-school teacher, don't simply ask that your class may be blessed, but pray for your children definitely by name before the Most High. And if there be a mercy in your household that you crave, don't go in a round-about way, but be simple and direct in your pleadings with God. When you pray to him, tell him what you want. If you have not money enough, if you are in poverty, if you are in straits, state the case. Use no mock-modesty with God. Come at once to the point; speak honestly with him. He needs no beautiful peniphrasis such as men will constantly use when they don't like to say right out what they mean. If you want either a temporal or spiritual mercy, say so. Don't ransack the Bible to find out words in which to express it. Express your wants in the words which naturally suggest themselves to you. They will be the best words, depend upon it. Abraham's words were the best for Abraham, and yours will be the best for you. You need not study all the texts in Scripture, to pray just as Jacob and Elias did, using their expressions. If you do you will not imitate them. You may imitate them literally and servilely, but you lack the soul that suggested and animated their words. Pray in your own words. Speak plainly to God; ask at once for what you want. Name persons, name things, and make a straight aim at the object of your supplications, and I am sure you will soon find that the weariness and dulness of which you often complain in your intercessions, will no more fall upon you; or at least not so habitually as it has heretofore done.

"But," saith one, "I do not feel that I have any special objects for which to pray." Ah! my dear brother, I know not who you are, or where you live, to be without special objects for prayer, for I find that every day brings either its need or its trouble, and that I have every day something to tell to my God. But if we had not a trouble, my dear brethren, if we had attained to such a height in grace that we had nothing to ask for, do we love Christ so much that we have no need to pray that we may love him more? Have we so much faith that we have ceased to cry, "Lord, increase it?" You will always, I am sure, by a little self-examination, soon discover that there is some legitimate object for which you may knock at Mercy's door and cry, "Give me, Lord, the desire of my heart." And if you have not any desire, you have but to ask the first tried Christian that you meet, and he will tell you of one. "Oh," he will reply to you, "if you have nothing to ask for yourself, pray for me. Ask that a sick wife may be recovered. Pray that the Lord would lift up the light of his countenance upon a heart; ask that the Lord would send help to some minister who has been labouring in vain, and spending his strength for nought." When you have done for yourself, plead for others; and if you cannot meet with one who can suggest a theme, look on this huge Sodom, this city like another Gomorrah lying before you; carry it constantly in your prayers before God and cry, "Oh that London may live before thee, that its sin may be stayed, that its righteousness may be exalted, that the God of the earth may get unto himself much people out of this city."

Equally necessary is it with a definite object for prayer that there should be an earnest desire for its attainment. "Cold prayers," says an old divine, "ask for a denial." When we ask the Lord coolly, and not fervently, we do as it were, stop his hand, and restrain him from giving us the very blessing we pretend that we are seeking. When you have your object in your eye, your soul must become so possessed with the value of that object, with your own excessive need for it, with the danger which you will be in unless that object should be granted, that you will be compelled to plead for it as a man pleadeth for his life. There was a beautiful illustration of true prayer addressed to man in the conduct of two noble ladies, whose husbands were condemned to die and were about to be executed, when they came before king George and supplicated for their pardon. The king rudely and cruelly repulsed them. George the first! it was like his very nature. And when they pleaded yet again, and again, and again, they could not be gotten to rise from their knees; they had actually to be dragged out of court, for they would not retire until the king had smiled upon them, and told them that their husbands should live. Alas! they failed, but they were noble women for their perseverance in thus pleading for their husbands' lives. That is the way for us to pray to God. We must have such a desire for the thing we want, that we will not rise until we have it—but in submission to his divine will, nevertheless. Feeling that the thing we ask for cannot be wrong, and that he himself hath promised it, we have resolved it must be given, and if not given, we will plead the promise, again, and again, till heaven's gates shall shake before our pleas shall cease. No wonder that God has not blessed us much of late, because we are not fervent in prayer as we should be. Oh, those cold-hearted prayers that die upon the lips—those frozen supplications; they do not move men's hearts, how should they move God's heart? they do not come from our own souls, they do not well up from the deep secret springs of our inmost heart, and therefore they cannot rise up to him who only hears the cry of the soul, before whom hypocrisy can weave no veil, or formality practise any disguise. We must be earnest, otherwise we have no right to hope that the Lord will hear our prayer.

And surely, my brethren, it were enough to restrain all lightness and constrain an unceasing earnestness, did we apprehend the greatness of the Being before whom we plead. Shall I come into thy presence, O my God, and mock thee with cold-hearted words? Do the angels veil their faces before thee, and shall I be content to prattle through a form with no soul and no heart? Ah, my brethren! we little know how many of our prayers are an abomination unto the Lord. It would be an abomination to you and to me to hear men ask us in the streets, as if they did not want what they asked for. But have we not done the same to God? Has not that which is heaven's greatest boon to man, become to us a dry dead duty? It was said of John Bradford that he had a peculiar art in prayer, and when asked for his secret he said, "When I know what I want I always stop on that prayer until I feel that I have pleaded it with God, and until God and I have had dealings with each other upon it." I never go on to another petition till I have gone through the first." Alas! for some men who begin "Our Father which art in heaven, hallowed be thy name;" and before they have realized the adoring thought—"hallowed be thy name,"—they have begun to repeat the next words—"Thy kingdom come;" then perhaps something strikes their mind, "Do I really wish his kingdom to come? If it were to come now where should I be?" And while they are thinking of that, their voice is going on with, "Thy will be done on earth as it is in heaven;" so they jumble up their prayers and run the sentences together. Oh! stop at each one till you have really prayed it. Do not try to put two arrows on the string at once, they will both miss. He that would load his gun with two charges, cannot expect to be successful. Discharge one shot first, and then load again. Plead once with God and prevail, and then plead again. Get the first mercy, and then go again for the second. Do not be satisfied with running the colours of your prayers into one another, till there is no picture to look at but just a huge daub, a smear of colours badly laid on. Look at the Lord's Prayer itself. What clear sharp outlines there are in it. There are certain definite mercies, and they do not run into one another. There it stands, and as you look at the whole it is a magnificent picture; not confusion, but beautiful order. Be it so with your prayers. Stay on one till you have prevailed with that, and then go on to the next. With definite objects and with fervent desires mixed together, there is the dawning of hope that ye shall prevail with God.

But again: these two things would not avail if they were not mixed with a still more essential and divine quality, namely, a firm faith in God. Brethren, do you believe in prayer? I know you pray because you are God's people; but do you believe in the power of prayer? There are a great many Christians that do not, they think it is a good thing, and they believe that sometimes it does wonders; but they do not think that prayer, real prayer, is always successful. They think that its effect depends upon many other things, but that it has not any essential quality or power in itself. Now, my own soul's conviction is, that prayer is the grandest power in the entire universe; that it has a more omnipotent force than electricity, attraction, gravitation, or any other of those secret forces which men have called by names, but which they do not understand. Prayer hath as palpable, as true, as sure, as invariable an influence over the entire universe as any of the laws of matter. When a man really prays, it is not a question whether God will hear him or not, he must hear him; not because there is any compulsion in the prayer, but there is a sweet and blessed compulsion in the promise. God has promised to hear prayer, and he will perform his promise. As he is the most high and true God, he cannot deny himself. Oh! to think of this; that you a puny man may stand here and speak to God, and through God may move all the worlds. Yet when your prayer is heard, creation will not be disturbed; though the grandest ends be answered, providence will not be disarranged for a single moment. Not a leaf will fall earlier from the tree, not a star will stay in its course, nor one drop of water trickle more slowly from its fount, all will go on the same, and yet your prayer will have effected everything. It will speak to the decrees and purposes of God, as they are being daily fulfilled; and they will all shout to your prayer, and cry, "Thou art our brother; we are decrees, and thou a prayer; but thou art thyself a decree, as old, as sure, as ancient as we are." Our prayers are God's decrees in another shape. The prayers of God's people are but God's promises breathed out of living hearts, and those promises are the decrees, only put into another form and fashion. Do not say, "How can my prayers affect the decrees?" They cannot, except in so much that your prayers are decrees, and that as they come out, every prayer that is inspired of the Holy Ghost unto your soul is as omnipotent and as eternal as that decree which said, "Let there be light, and there was light;" or as that decree which chose his people, and ordained their redemption by the precious blood of Christ. Thou hast power in prayer, and thou standest to-day among the most potent ministers in the universe that God has made. Thou hast power over angels, they will fly at thy will. Thou hast power over fire, and water, and the elements of earth. Thou hast power to make thy voice heard beyond the stars; where the thunders die out in silence, thy voice shall wake the echoes of eternity. The ear of God himself shall listen and the hand of God himself shall yield to thy will. He bids thee cry, "Thy will be done," and thy will shall be done. When thou canst plead his promise then thy will is his will. Seems it not my dear friends, an awful thing to have such a power in one's hands as to be able to pray? You have heard sometimes of men who pretended to have a weird and mystic might, by which they could call up spirits from the vasty deep, by which they could make showers of rain, or stop the sun. It was all a figment of the fancy, but were it true the Christian is a greater magician still. If he has but faith in God, there is nothing impossible to him. He shall be delivered out of the deepest waters—he shall be rescued out of the sorest troubles—in famine he shall be fed—in pestilence he shall go unscathed—amidst calamity he shall walk firm and strong—in war he shall be ever shielded—and in the day of battle he shall lift up his head, if he can but believe the promise, and hold it up before God's eyes and plead it with the spell of unfaltering reliance. There is nothing, I repeat it, there is no force so tremendous, no energy so marvellous, as the energy with which God has endowed every man, who like Jacob can wrestle, like Israel can prevail with him in prayer. But we must have faith in this; we must believe prayer to be what it is, or else it is not what it should be. Unless I believe my prayer to be effectual it will not be, for on my faith will it to a great extent depend. God may give me the mercy even when I have not faith; that will be his own sovereign grace, but he has not promised to do it. But when I have faith and can plead the promise with earnest desire, it is no longer a probability as to whether I shall get the blessing, or whether my will shall be done. Unless the Eternal will swerve from his Word, unless the oath which he has given shall be revoked, and he himself shall cease to be what he is, "We know that we have the petitions that we desired of him."

And now to mount one step higher, together with definite objects, fervent desires and strong faith in the efficacy of prayer there should be—and Oh may divine grace make it so with us!—there should be mingled a realising expectation. We should be able to count over the mercies before we have got them, believing that they are on the road. Reading the other day in a sweet little book, which I would commend to the attention of you all, written by an American author who seems to know the power of prayer thoroughly, and to whom I am indebted for many good things—a little book called *The Still Hour*, I met with a reference to a passage in the book of Daniel, the tenth chapter I think. where, as he says, the whole machinery of prayer seems to be laid bare. Daniel is on his knees in prayer, and Michael the archangel comes to him. He talks with him and tells him that as soon as ever Daniel began to set his heart to understand, and to chasten himself before God, his words were heard, and the Lord had despatched the angel. Then he tells him in the most business-like manner in the world, "I should have been here before, but the Prince of Persia withstood me; nevertheless the prince of thy nation helped me, and I am come to comfort and instruct thee." See now, God breathes the desire into our hearts, and as soon as the desire is there, before we call he begins to answer. Before the words have got half way up to heaven, while they are yet trembling on the lip— knowing the words we mean to speak—he begins to answer them, sends the angel; the angel comes and brings down the needed blessing. Why the thing is a revelation if you could see it with your eyes. Some people think that spiritual things are dreams, and that we are talking fancies. Nay, I do believe there is as much reality in a Christian's prayer as in a lightning flash; and the utility and excellency of the prayer of a Christian may be just as sensibly known as the power of the lightning flash when it rends the tree, breaks off its branches; and splits it to the very root. Prayer is not a fancy or fiction; it is a real actual thing, coercing the universe, binding the laws of God themselves in fetters, and constraining the High and Holy One to listen to the will of his poor but favoured creature-man. But we want always to believe this. We need a realizing assurance in prayer. To count over the mercies before they are come! To be sure that they are coming! To act as if we had got them! When you have asked for your daily bread, no more to be disturbed with care, but to believe that God has heard you, and will give it to you. When you have taken the case of your sick child, before God to believe that the child will recover, or if it should not that it will be a greater blessing to you and more glory to God, and so to leave it to him. To be able to say, "I know he has heard me now; I will stand on my watchtower; I will look for my God and hear what he will say to my soul." Were you ever disappointed yet, Christian, when you prayed in faith and expected the answer? I bear my own testimony here this morning, that I have never yet trusted him and found him fail me. I have trusted man and have been deceived, but my God has never once denied the request I have made to him, when I have backed up the request with belief in his willingness to hear, and in the assurance of his promise.

But I hear some one say, "May we pray for temporals?" Ay, that you may. In everything make known your wants to God. It is not merely for spiritual, but for everyday concerns. Take your smallest trials before him. He is a God that heareth prayer; he is your household God as well as the God of the sanctuary. Be ever taking all that you have before God. As one good man who is about to be united with this Church told me of his departed wife, "Oh," said he, "she was a woman that I could never get to do anything till she had made a matter of prayer of it. Be it what it might, she used to say, 'I must make it a matter of prayer;'" Oh for more o this sweet habit of spreading everything before the Lord, just as Hezekiah did Rabshekah's letter, and there leaving it, saying, "Thy will be done, I resign it to thee! Men say Mr. Müller of Bristol is enthusiastic, because he will gather seven hundred children and believe that God will provide for them; though there is nothing in the purse oftentimes, yet he believes it will come. My dear brethren, he is not an enthusiast; he is only doing what ought to be the commonplace action of every Christian man. He is acting upon a rule at which the worldling always must scoff, because he does not understand it; a system which must always appear to the weak judgment of sense, visionary and romantic, but which will never appear so to the child of God. He acts not upon common sense, but upon something higher than common sense—upon uncommon faith. Oh that we had that uncommon faith to take God at his word! He cannot and he will not permit the man that trusteth him to be ashamed or confounded. I have thus now, as best I could, set forth before you what I conceive to be four essentials of prevailing prayer—"Whatsoever things ye desire when ye pray, believe that ye receive them and ye shall have them."

II. Having thus asked you to look at the text, I want you now to LOOK ABOUT YOU. Look about you at our meetings for prayer, and look about you at your private intercessions, and judge them both by the tenour of this text. First, look about you at the meetings for prayer; I cannot speak very pointedly in this matter, because I do honestly believe that the prayer-meetings which are usually held among us, have far less of the faults which I am about to indicate, than any others I have ever attended. But, still they have some of the faults, and I hope that what we shall say, will be taken personally home by every brother who is in the habit of engaging publicly in supplication at prayer-meetings. Is it not a fact, that as soon as you enter the meeting, you feel, that if you are called upon to pray, you have to exercise a gift. And that gift, in the case of many praying men (to speak hardly perhaps, but I think honestly) lies in having a good memory to recollect a great many texts, which always have been quoted since the days of our grandfather's grandfather, and to be able to repeat them in good regular order. The gift lies also in some churches, especially in village churches, in having strong lungs, so as to be able to hold out, without taking breath for five and twenty minutes when you are brief, and three quarters of an hour when you are rather drawn out. The gift lies also in being able not to ask for anything in particular, but in passing through a range of everything, making the prayer, not an arrow with a point, but rather like a nondescript machine, that has no point whatever, and yet is meant to be all point, which is aimed at everything, and consequently strikes nothing. Those brethren are often the most frequently asked to pray, who have those peculiar, and perhaps, excellent gifts, although I certainly must say that I cannot obey the apostle's injunction in coveting very earnestly such gifts as these. Now, if, instead thereof, some man is asked to pray, who has never prayed before in public; suppose he rises and says, "*Oh Lord, I feel myself such a sinner that I can scarcely speak to thee, Lord, help me to pray! O Lord, save my poor soul! O that thou wouldst save my old companions! Lord, bless our minister! be pleased to give us a revival. O Lord, I can say no more; hear me for Jesu's sake! Amen.*" Well, then, you feel somehow, as if you had begun to pray yourself. You feel an interest in that man, partly from fear lest he should stop, and also because you are sure that what he did say, he meant. And if another should get up after that, and pray in the same spirit, you go out and say, "This is real prayer." I would sooner have three minutes, prayer like that, than thirty minutes of the other sort, because the one is praying, and the other is preaching. Allow me to quote what an old preacher said upon the subject of prayer, and give it to you as a little word of advice—"Remember, the Lord will not hear thee, because of the *arithmetic* of thy prayers; he does not count their numbers. He will not hear thee because of the *rhetoric* of thy prayers; he does not care for the eloquent language in which they are conveyed. He will not listen to thee because of the *geometry* of thy prayers; he does not compute them by their length, or by their breadth. He will not regard thee because of the *music* of thy prayers; he doth not care for sweet voices, nor for harmonious periods. Neither will he look at thee because of the *logic* of thy prayers; because they are well arranged, and excellently comparted. But he will hear thee, and he will measure the amount of the blessing he will give thee, according to the *divinity* of thy prayers. If thou canst plead the person of Christ, and if the Holy Ghost inspire thee with zeal and earnestness, the blessings which thou shalt ask, shall surely come unto thee." Brethren, I would like to burn the whole stock of old prayers that we have been using this fifty years. That "oil that goes from vessel to vessel,"—that "horse that rushes into the battle,"—that misquoted mangled text, "where two or three are met together, thou wilt be in the midst of them, and that to bless them,"— and all those other quotations which we have been manufacturing, and dislocating, and copying from man to man. I would we came to speak to God, just out of our own hearts. It would be a grand thing for our prayer meetings; they would be better attended; and I am sure they would be more fruitful, if every man would shake off that habit of formality, and talk to God as a child talks to his father; ask him for what we want, and then sit down and have done. I say this with all Christian earnestness. Often, because I have not chosen to pray in any convential form, people have said, "That man is not reverent!" My dear sir, you are not a judge of my reverence. To my own master, I stand or fall. I do not think that Job quoted anybody. I do not think that Jacob quoted the old saint in heaven,—his father Abraham. I do not find Jesus Christ quoted Scripture in prayer. They did not pray in other people's words, but they prayed in their own. God does not want you to go gathering up those excellent but very musty spices of the old sanctuary. He wants the new oil just distilled from the fresh olive of your own soul. He wants spices and frankincense, not of the old chests, where they have been lying until they have lost their savour, but he wants fresh incense, and fresh myrrh, brought from the ophir of your own soul's experience. Look well to it that you really pray, do not learn the language of prayer, but seek the spirit of prayer, and God Almighty bless you, and make you more mighty in your supplications.

I have said, "Look about you." I want you to continue the work, and look about at your own closets. Oh! brethren and sisters, there is no place that some of us need to be so much ashamed to look at as our closet door. I cannot say the hinges are rusty; they do open and shut at their appointed seasons. I cannot say that the door is locked and cobwebbed. We do not neglect prayer itself; but those walls, those beams out of the wall, what a tale might they tell! "Oh!" the wall might cry out, "I have heard thee when thou hast been in so vast a hurry that thou couldst scarcely spend two minutes with thy God, and I have heard thee, too, when thou wast neither asleep nor awake, and when thou didst not know what thou wast saying." Then one beam might cry out, "I have heard thee come and spend ten minutes and not ask for anything, at least thy heart did not ask. The lips moved, but the heart was silent." How might another beam cry out—"Oh! I have heard thee groan out thy soul, but I have seen thee go away distrustful, not believing thy prayer was heard, quoting the promise, but not thinking God would fulfil it." Surely the four walls of the closet might come together and fall down upon us in their anger, because we have so often insulted God with our unbelief and with our hurry, and with all manner of sins. We have insulted him even at his mercy seat, on the spot where his condescension is most fully manifested. Is it not so with you? Must we not each confess it in our turn? See to it then, Christian brethren, that an amendment be made, and God make you more mighty and more successful in your prayers than heretofore.

III. But not to detain you, the last point is, look upward, look above. LOOK ABOVE. Christian brethren and sisters, and let us weep. Oh God, thou hast given us a mighty weapon, and we have permitted it to rust. Thou hast given us that which is mighty as thyself, and we have let that power lie dormant. Would it not be a vile crime if a man had an eye given him which he would not open, or a hand that he would not lift up, or a foot that grew stiff because he would not use it. And what must we say of ourselves when God has given us power in prayer, matchless power, full of blessedness to ourselves, and of unnumbered mercies to others, and yet that power lies still. Oh, if the universe was as still as we are, where should we be? Oh God, thou givest light to the sun and he shines with it. Thou givest light even to the stars and they twinkle. To the winds thou givest force and they blow. And to the air thou givest life and it moves, and men breathe thereof. But to thy people thou hast given a gift that is better than force, and life, and light, and yet they permit it to lie still. Forgetful almost that they wield the power, seldom exercising it, though it would be blessed to countless myriads. Weep, Christian man. Constantine, the Emperor of Rome, saw that on the coins of the other Emperors, their images were in an erect posture—triumphing. Instead thereof he ordered that his image should be struck kneeling, for said he—"That is the way in which I have triumphed." We shall never triumph till our image is struck kneeling. The reason why we have been defeated, and why our banners trail in the dust, is because we have not prayed. Go—go ye back to your God, with sorrow, confess before him, ye children of Ephraim, that ye were armed, and carried bows, but turned your backs in the day of battle. Go to your God and tell him that if souls are not saved, it is not because he has not power to save, but because you have never travailed as it were in birth for perishing sinners. Your bowels have not sounded like a harp for Kir-haresh, neither has your spirit been moved, because of the defences of the tribe of Reuben. Wake up, wake up, ye people of Israel; be astonished, ye careless ones; ye who have neglected prayer; ye sinners that are in Zion's own self, and that have been at ease. Wake up yourselves; wrestle and strive with your God, and then the blessing shall come-the early and the latter rain of his mercy, and the earth shall bring forth plenteously, and all the nations shall call him blessed. Look up then, and weep.

Once more look up and rejoice. Though you have sinned against him he loves you still. Ye have not prayed unto him nor sought his face, but behold he cries to you still—"Seek ye my face;" and he saith not "Seek ye me in vain." Ye may not have gone to the fountain, but it flows as freely as before. Ye have shut your eye to that sun, but it still shines upon you with all its lustre. Ye have not drawn near to God, but he waiteth to be gracious still, and is ready to hear all your petitions. Behold, he says uuto you, "Enquire of me concerning things to come, and concerning my sons and daughters, command ye me." What a blessed thing it is that the master in heaven is always ready to hear! Augustine has a very beautiful thought upon the parable of the man who knocked at his friend's door at midnight, saying, "Friend, give me three loaves." His paraphrase of it runs something like this—I knock at mercy's door, and it is the dead of night. "Will not some of the servants of the house come and answer me?" No; I knock, but they are asleep. Oh! ye apostles of God—ye glorified martyrs—ye are asleep; ye rest in your beds; ye cannot hear my prayer. But will not the children answer? Are there not children who are ready to come and open the door to their brother? No; they are asleep. My brethren that have departed—with whom I took sweet counsel, and who were the companions of my heart—ye cannot answer me for ye rest in Jesus; your works do follow you, but you cannot work for me. But while the servants are asleep, and while the children cannot answer, the Master is awake,—awake at midnight too. It may be midnight with my soul, but he hears me, and when I am saying "Give me three loaves," he comes to the door and giveth me as much as I need. Christian, look up then and rejoice. There is always an open ear if you have an open mouth. There is always a ready hand if you have a ready heart. You have but to cry and the Lord hears; nay, before you call he will answer, and while you are speaking he will hear. Oh! be not backward then in prayer. Go to him when you reach your home; nay, on the very way lift up your hearts silently; and whatever your petition or request may be, ask it in Jesu's name, and it shall be done unto you.

Yet, again, look up, dear Christian brethren, and amend your prayers from this time forth. Look on pvayer no longer as a romantic fiction or as an arduous duty; look at it as a real power, as a real pleasure. When philosophers discover some latent power, they seem to have a delight to put it in action. I believe there have been many great engineers, who have designed and constructed some of the most wonderful of human works, not because they would be remunerative, but simply from a love of showing their own power to accomplish wonders. To show the world what skill could do and what man could accomplish, they have tempted companies into speculations that could never remunerate apparently, so far as I could see, in order that they might have an opportunity of displaying their genius. O Christian men, and shall a great Engineer attempt great works and display his power, and will you who have a mightier power than ever was wielded by any man apart from his God—will you let that be still? Nay think of some great object, strain the sinews of your supplication for it. Let every vein of your heart be full to the brim with the rich blood of desire, and struggle, and wrestle, and tug and strive with God for it, using the promises and pleading the attributes, and see if God does not give you your heart's desire. I challenge you this day to exceed in prayer my Master's bounty. I throw down the gauntlet to you. Believe him to be more than he is; open your mouth so wide that he cannot fill it; go to him now for more faith than the promise warrants; venture it, risk it, outdo the Eternal if it be possible; attempt it. Or as I would rather put it thus, take your petitions and wants and see if he does not honor you. Try whether if you believe him he doth not fulfil the promise, and richly bless you with the anointing oil of his Spirit by which you will be strong in prayer.

I cannot refrain from adding just these few syllables as you go away. I know there are some of you that never prayed in your lives. You have said a form of prayer, perhaps, many years, but have never prayed once. Ah! poor soul, you must be born again, and until you are born again you cannot pray as I have been directing the Christian to pray. But let me say this much to you. Does your heart long after salvation? Has the Spirit whispered, "Come to Jesus, sinner, he will hear you?" Believe that whisper, for he will hear you. The prayer of the awakened sinner is acceptable to God. He heareth the broken in heart and healeth them too. Take your groans and your sighs to God and he will answer you. "Ah," but says one, "I have nothing to plead." Well, but plead as David did—"Pardon my iniquity, for it is great." You have that plea—your iniquity is very great Then plead that precious blood—that all prevailing plea—say, "For his dear sake who shed his blood," and you shall prevail, sinner. But do not go to God, and ask for mercy with thy sin in thy hand. What would you think of the rebel, who appeared before the face of his sovereign and asked for pardon with the dagger sticking in his belt, and with the declaration of his rebellion on his breast? Would he deserve to be pardoned? He could not deserve it in any case, and surely he would deserve double his doom for having thus mocked his master while he pretended to be seeking mercy. If a wife had forsaken her husband do you think she would have the impudence, with brazen forehead, to come back and ask his pardon leaning on the arm of her paramour? No, she could not have such impudence, and yet it is so with you—perhaps asking for mercy and going on in sin—praying to be reconciled to God, and yet harbouring and indulging your lust. Awake! awake! and call upon thy God, thou sleeper. The boat is nearing the rock, perhaps to-morrow it may strike and be shivered, and thou be cast into the unfathomable depths of everlasting woe. Call on thy God, I say, and when thou callest upon him, cast away thy sin or he cannot hear thee. If thou lift up thy unholy hands with a lie in thy right hand, a prayer is worthless on thy lip. Oh, come unto him, say unto him, Take away all iniquity, receive us graciously, love us freely," and he will hear you, and you shall yet pray as prevailing princes, and one day shall stand as more than conquerors before the starry throne of him who ever reigns God over all, blessed for evermore.

2
THE SECRET OF POWER IN PRAYER

"If ye abide in me, and my words abide in you, ye shall ask what ye will, and it shall be done unto you."—John 15:7

"Satan trembles when he sees the weakest saint upon his knees."
— *William Cowper*

~

THE gifts of grace are not enjoyed all at once by believers. Coming unto Christ, we are saved by a true union with him; but it is by abiding in that union that we further receive the purity, the joy, the power, the blessedness, which are stored up in him for his people. See how our Lord states this when he speaks to the believing Jews in the eighth chapter of this gospel, at the thirty-first and thirty-second verses:— "Then said Jesus to those Jews which believed on him, If ye continue in my word, then are ye my disciples indeed; and ye shall know the truth, and the truth shall make you free." We do not know all the truth at once: we learn it by abiding in Jesus.

Perseverance in grace is an educational process by which we learn the truth fully. The emancipating power of that truth is also gradually perceived and enjoyed. "The truth shall make you free." One bond after another snaps, and we are free indeed. You that are young beginners in the divine life may be cheered to know that there is something better still for you: you have not yet received the full recompense of your faith. As your hymn puts it—"It is better on before." You shall have happier views of heavenly things as you climb the hill of spiritual experience. As you abide in Christ you shall have firmer confidence, richer joy, greater stability, more communion with Jesus, and greater delight in the Lord your God. Infancy is beset with many evils from which manhood is exempt: it is the same in the spiritual as in the natural world.

There are these degrees of attainment among believers, and the Saviour here incites us to reach a high position by mentioning a certain privilege which is not for all who say that they are in Christ, but for those only who are *abiders* in him. Every believer should be an abider, but many have hardly earned the name as yet. Jesus says, "If ye abide in me, and my words abide in you, ye shall ask what ye will, and it shall be done unto you." You have to live with Christ to know him, and the longer you live with him the more will you admire and adore him; yes, and the more will you receive from him, even grace for grace. Truly he is a blessed Christ to one who is but a month old in grace; but these babes can hardly tell what a precious Jesus he is to those whose acquaintance with him covers well-nigh half a century! Jesus, in the esteem of abiding believers, grows sweeter and dearer, fairer and more lovely, day by day. Not that he improves in himself, for he is perfect; but that as we increase in our knowledge of him, we appreciate more thoroughly his matchless excellences. How glowingly do his old acquaintances exclaim, "Yea, he is altogether lovely"! Oh, that we may continue to grow up into him in all things who is our head, that we thus may prize him more and more!

I call your earnest attention to our text, begging you to consider with me three questions. First, *what is this special blessing?* "Ye shall ask what ye will, and it shall be done unto you." Secondly, *how is this special blessing obtained?* "If ye abide in me, and my words abide in you." Then, thirdly, *why is it obtained in this way?* There must be a reason for the conditions laid down as needful to obtaining the promised power in prayer. Oh, that the anointing of the Holy Spirit which abideth on us may now make this subject very profitable to us!

I. WHAT IS THIS SPECIAL BLESSING? Let us read the verse again. Jesus says, "If ye abide in me, and my words abide in you, ye shall ask what ye will, and it shall be done unto you."

Observe that our Lord had been warning us that, severed from him, we can do nothing, and, therefore, we might naturally have expected that he would now show us how we can do all spiritual acts. But the text does not run as we should have expected it to run. The Lord Jesus does not say, "Without me ye can do nothing, but, if ye abide in me, and my words abide in you, ye shall do all spiritual and gracious things." He does not now speak of what they should themselves be enabled to do, but of what should be done unto them: "it shall be done unto you." He says not,

"Strength shall be given you sufficient for all those holy doings of which you are incapable apart from me." That would have been true enough, and it is the truth which we looked for here; but our most wise Lord improves upon all parallelisms of speech, and improves upon all expectancies of heart, and says something better still. He does not say, "If ye abide in me, and my words abide in you, ye shall do spiritual things"; but, "ye shall ask." By prayer you shall be enabled to do; but before all attempts to do, "Ye shall ask." The choice privilege here given is a mighty prevailing prayerfulness. Power in prayer is very much the gauge of our spiritual condition; and when that is secured to us in a high degree, we are favoured as to all other matters.

One of the first results, then, of our abiding union with Christ will be *the certain exercise of prayer:* "Ye shall ask." If others neither seek, nor knock, nor ask, ye, at any rate, shall do so. Those who keep away from Jesus do not pray. Those in whom communion with Christ is suspended feel as if they could not pray; but Jesus says, "If ye abide in me, and my words abide in you, ye shall ask." Prayer comes spontaneously from those who abide in Jesus, even as certain oriental trees, without pressure, shed their fragrant gums. Prayer is the natural outgushing of a soul in communion with Jesus. Just as the leaf and the fruit will come out of the vine-branch without any conscious effort on the part of the branch, but simply because of its living union with the stem, so prayer buds, and blossoms, and fruits out of souls abiding in Jesus. As stars shine, so do abiders pray. It is their use and their second nature. They do not say to themselves, "Now it is the time for us to get to our task and pray." No, they pray as wise men eat, namely, when the desire for it is upon them. They do not cry out as under bondage, "At this time I ought to be in prayer, but I do not feel like it. What a weariness it is!" but they have a glad errand at the mercy-seat, and they are rejoiced to go upon it. Hearts abiding in Christ send forth supplications as fires send out flames and sparks. Souls abiding in Jesus open the day with prayer; prayer surrounds them as an atmosphere all day long; at night they fall asleep praying. I have known them even dream a prayer, and, at any rate, they are able joyfully to say, "When I awake, I am still with thee." Habitual asking comes out of abiding in Christ. You will not need urging to prayer when you are abiding with Jesus: he says, "Ye shall ask"; and, depend upon it, you will.

You shall also feel most powerfully *the necessity of prayer.* Your great need of prayer will be vividly seen. Do I hear you say—"What! When we abide in Christ, and his words abide in us, have we not already attained?" Far are we, then, from being satisfied with ourselves; it is then that we feel more than ever that we must ask for more grace. He that knows Christ best, knows his own necessities best. He that is most conscious of life in Christ, is also most convinced of his own death apart from Christ. He who most clearly discerns the perfect character of Jesus, will be most urgent in prayer for grace to grow like him. The more I see to be in my Lord, the more I desire to obtain from him, since I know that all that is in him is put there on purpose that I may receive it. "Of his fulness have all we received, and grace for grace." It is just in proportion as we are linked to Christ's fulness that we feel the necessity of drawing from it by constant prayer. Nobody needs to prove to an abider in Christ the doctrine of prayer, for we enjoy the thing itself. Prayer is now as much a necessity of our spiritual life as breath is of our natural life: we cannot live without asking favours of the Lord. "If ye abide in me, and my words abide in you, ye *shall* ask": and ye shall not wish to cease from asking. He hath said, "Seek ye my face," and your heart will answer, "Thy face, Lord, will I seek."

Note next, that the fruit of our abiding is not only the exercise of prayer, and a sense of the necessity of prayer, but it includes *liberty in prayer*: "Ye shall ask what ye will." Have you not been on your knees at times without power to pray? Have you not felt that you could not plead as you desired? You wanted to pray, but the waters were frozen up, and would not flow. You said, mournfully, "I am shut up, and cannot come forth." The will was present, but not the freedom to present that will in prayer. Do you, then, desire liberty in prayer, so that you may speak with God as a man speaketh with his friend? Here is the way to it: "If ye abide in me, and my words abide in you, ye shall ask what ye will." I do not mean that you will gain liberty as to mere fluency of utterance, for that is a very inferior gift. Fluency is a questionable endowment, especially when it is not attended with weight of thought and depth of feeling. Some brethren pray by the yard; but true prayer is measured by weight, and not by length. A single groan before God may have more fulness of prayer in it than a fine oration of great length. He that dwells with God in Christ Jesus, he is the man whose steps are enlarged in intercession. He comes boldly because he abides at the throne. He sees the golden sceptre stretched out, and hears the King saying, "Ask what thou wilt, and it shall be done unto thee." It is the man who abides in conscious union with his Lord who has freedom of access in prayer. Well may he come to Christ readily, for he is in Christ, and abides in him. Attempt not to seize this holy liberty by excitement, or presumption: there is but one way of really gaining it, and here it is—"If ye abide in me, and my words abide in you, ye shall ask what ye will." By this means alone shall you be enabled to open your mouth wide, that God may fill it. Thus shall you become Israels, and as princes have power with God.

This is not all: the favoured man has the privilege of *successful prayer.* "Ye shall ask what ye will, and it shall be done unto you." You may not do it, but it shall be done unto you. You long to bear fruit: ask, and it shall be done unto you. Look at the vine branch. It simply remains in the vine, and by remaining in the vine the fruit comes from it; it is done unto it. Brother in Christ, the purport of your being, its one object and design, is to bring forth fruit to the glory of the Father: to gain this end you must abide in Christ, as the branch abides in the vine. This is the method by which your prayer for fruitfulness will become successful, "it shall be done unto you." Concerning this matter, "you shall ask what you will, and it shall be done unto you." You shall have wonderful prevalence with God in prayer, insomuch that before you call he will answer, and while you are yet speaking he will hear. "The desire of the righteous shall be granted." To the same effect is the other text: "Delight thyself also in the Lord; and he shall give thee the desires of thine heart." There is a great breadth in this text, "Ye shall ask what ye will, and it shall be done unto you." The Lord gives the abider *carte blanche*. He puts into his hand a signed cheque, and permits him to fill it up as he wills.

Does the text mean what it says? I never knew my Lord to say anything he did not mean. I am sure that he may sometimes mean more than we understand him to say, but he never means less. Mind you, he does not say to all men, "I will give you whatever you ask." Oh no, that would be an unkind kindness: but he speaks to his disciples, and says, "If ye abide in me, and my words abide in you, ye shall ask what ye will, and it shall be done unto you." It is to a certain class of men who have already received great grace at his hands—it is to them he commits this marvellous power of prayer. O my dear friends, if I may covet earnestly one thing above every other, it is this; that I may be able to ask what I will of the Lord, and have it. The prevailer in prayer is the man to preach successfully, for he may well prevail with man for God when he has already prevailed with God for men. This is the man to face the difficulties of business life; for what can baffle him when he can take all to God in prayer? One such man as this, or one such woman as this in a church, is worth ten thousand of us common people. In these we find the peerage of the skies. In these are the men in whom is fulfilled God's purpose concerning man, whom he made to have dominion over all the works of his hands. The stamp of sovereignty is on the brows of these men: they shape the history of nations, they guide the current of events through their power on high. We see Jesus with all things put under him by the divine purpose, and as we rise into that image, we also are clothed with dominion, and are made kings and priests unto God. Behold Elijah, with the keys of the rain swinging at his girdle: he shuts or opens the windows of heaven! There are such men still alive. Aspire to be such men and women, I beseech you, that to you the text may be fulfilled. "Ye shall ask what ye will, and it shall be done unto you."

The text seems to imply that, if we reach this point of privilege, this gift shall be a perpetuity: "Ye shall ask," ye shall always ask; ye shall never get beyond asking, but ye shall ask successfully, for "ye shall ask what ye will, and it shall be done unto you." Here we have the gift of *continual prayer*. Not for the week of prayer, not during a month's conference, nor upon a few special occasions shall ye pray prevailingly; but ye shall possess this power with God so long as you abide in Christ, and his words abide in you. God will put his omnipotence at your disposal: he will put forth his Godhead to fulfil the desires which his own Spirit has inwrought in you. I wish I could make this jewel glitter before the eyes of all the saints till they cried out, "Oh that we had it!" This power in prayer is like the sword of Goliath: wisely may every David say—"There is none like it; give it me." This weapon of all-prayer beats the enemy, and, at the same time, enriches its possessor with all the wealth of God. How can he lack anything to whom the Lord hath said, "Ask what thou wilt, and it shall be done unto thee"? Oh, come, let us seek this boon. Listen, and learn the way. Follow me, while by the light of the text I point out the path. May the Lord lead us in it by his Holy Spirit!

II. The privilege of mighty prayerfulness—HOW IS IT TO BE OBTAINED? The answer is, "If ye abide in me, and my words abide in you." Here are the two feet by which we climb to power with God in prayer.

Beloved, the first line tells us that we are to *abide in Christ Jesus our Lord*. It is taken for granted that we are already in him. May it be taken for granted in your case, dear hearer? If so, you are to abide where you are. As believers we are to remain tenaciously clinging to Jesus, livingly knit to Jesus. We are to abide in him, by always trusting him, and him only, with the same simple faith which joined us to him at the first. We must never admit any other thing or person into our heart's confidence as our hope of salvation, but rest alone in Jesus as we received him at the first. His Godhead, his manhood, his life, his death, his resurrection, his glory at the right hand of the Father—in a word, himself must be our heart's sole reliance. This is absolutely essential. A temporary faith will not save: an abiding faith is needful.

But abiding in the Lord Jesus does not only mean trusting in him; it includes our yielding ourselves up to him to receive his life, and to let that life work out its results in us. We live *in* him, *by* him, *for* him, *to* him, when we abide in him. We feel that all our separate life has gone: for "ye are dead, and your life is hid with Christ." We are nothing if we get away from Jesus; we should then be branches withered, and fit only to be cast into the fire. We have no reason for existence except that which we find in Christ; and what a marvellous reason that is! The vine needs the branch as truly as the branch needs the vine. No vine ever bore any fruit except upon its branches. Truly it bears all the branches, and so bears all the fruit; but yet it is by the branch that the vine displays its fruitfulness. Thus are abiding believers needful to the fulfilment of their Lord's design. Wonderful thing to

CHARLES SPURGEON

say; but the saints are needful to their Saviour! The church is his body; the fulness of him that filleth all in all. I want you to recognize this, that you may see your blessed responsibility, your practical obligation to bring forth fruit, that the Lord Jesus may be glorified in you. Abide in him. Never remove from your consecration to his honour and glory. Never dream of being your own master. Be not the servant of men, but abide in Christ. Let him be the object, as well as the source, of your existence. Oh, if you get there, and stop there in perpetual communion with your Lord, you will soon realize a joy, a delight, a power in prayer, such as you never knew before. There are times when we are conscious that we are in Christ, and we know our fellowship with him; and oh, the joy and the peace which we drink from this cup! Let us abide there. "Abide in me," saith Jesus. You are not to come and go, but to abide. Let that blessed sinking of yourself into his life, the spending of all your powers for Jesus, and the firm faith of your union with him remain in you evermore. Oh, that we might attain to this by the Holy Ghost!

As if to help us to understand this, our gracious Lord has given us a delightful parable. Let us look through this discourse of the vine and its branches. Jesus says, "Every branch in me that beareth fruit, he purgeth it." Take care that you *abide in Christ when you are being purged.* "Oh," says one, "I thought I was a Christian; but, alas! I have more troubles than ever: men ridicule me, the devil tempts me, and my business affairs go wrong." Brother, if you are to have power in prayer you must take care that you abide in Christ when the sharp knife is cutting everything away. Endure trial, and never dream of giving up your faith because of it. Say, "Though he slay me, yet will I trust in him." Your Lord warned you when you first came into the vine that you would have to be purged and cut closely; and if you are now feeling the purging process, you must not think that some strange thing hath happened unto you. Rebel not because of anything you may have to suffer from the dear hand of your heavenly Father, who is the husbandman of the vineyard. No, but cling to Jesus all the more closely. Say, "Cut, Lord, cut to the quick if thou wilt; but I will cling to thee. To whom should we go? Thou hast the words of eternal life." Yes, cling to Jesus when the purging knife is in his hand, and so "shall ye ask what ye will, and it shall be done unto you."

Take care, also, that *when the purging operation has been carried out you still cleave to your Lord.* Notice the third verse: "Now ye are clean through the word which I have spoken unto you. Abide in me, and I in you." Abide after cleansing where you were before cleansing. When you are sanctified, abide where you were when first justified. When you see the work of the Spirit increasing in you, do not let the devil tempt you to boast that now you are somebody, and need not come to Jesus as a poor sinner, and rest in his precious blood alone for salvation. Abide still in Jesus. As you kept to him when the knife cut you, keep to him now that the tender grapes begin to form. Do not say to yourself, "What a fruitful branch I am! How greatly I adorn the vine! Now I am full of vigour!" You are nothing and nobody. Only as you abide in Christ are you one whit better than the waste wood which is burned in the fire. "But do we not make progress?" Yes, we grow, but we abide: we never go an inch further, we abide in him; or, if not, we are cast forth, and are withered. Our whole hope lies in Jesus at our best times as well as at our worst. Jesus saith, "Now ye are clean through the word which I have spoken unto you. Abide in me, and I in you."

Abide in him *as to all your fruitfulness.* "As the branch cannot bear fruit of itself except it abide in the vine, no more can ye, except ye abide in me." "Here, then, I have something to do," cries one. Certainly you have, but not apart from Jesus. The branch has to bear fruit; but if the branch imagines that it is going to produce a cluster, or even a grape, out of itself alone, it is utterly mistaken. The fruit of the branch must come forth of the stem. Your work for Christ must be Christ's work in you, or else it will be good for nothing. I pray you, see to this. Your Sunday-school teaching, your preaching, or whatever you do, must be done in Christ Jesus. Not by your natural talent can you win souls, nor by plans of your own inventing can you save men. Beware of home-made schemes. Do for Jesus what Jesus bids you do. Remember that our work for Christ, as we call it, must be Christ's work first, if it is to be accepted of him. Abide in him as to your fruit-bearing.

Yea, abide in him *as to your very life.* Do not say, "I have been a Christian man now twenty or thirty years, I can do without continued dependence upon Christ." No, you could not do without him if you were as old as Methuselah. Your very being as a Christian depends upon your still clinging, still trusting, still depending; and this he must give you, for it all comes from him, and him alone. To sum it all up, if you want that splendid power in prayer of which I spoke just now, you must remain in loving, living, lasting, conscious, practical, abiding union with the Lord Jesus Christ; and if you get to that by divine grace, then you shall ask what you will, and it shall be done unto you.

But there is a second qualification mentioned in the text, and you must not forget it—"*and my words abide in you.*" How important, then, are Christ's words! He said in the fourth verse, "Abide in me, and I in you," and now as a parallel to this it is, "If ye abide in me, and my words abide in you." What, then, are Christ's words and himself identical? Yes, practically so. Some talk about Christ being the Master, but as to doctrine, they do not care what his word declares. So long as their hearts are right towards his person they claim liberty of thought. Ay, but this is a mere subterfuge. We cannot separate Christ from the Word; for, in the first place, he is the Word; and, in the next place, how dare we call him Master and Lord and do not the things which he says, and reject the truth which he teaches? We must obey his precepts or he will not accept us as disciples. Especially that precept of love which is the essence of all his words. We must love God and our brethren; yea, we must cherish love to all men, and seek their good. Anger and malice must be far from us. We must walk even as he walked. If Christ's words abide not in thee, both as to belief and practice, thou art not in Christ. Christ and his gospel and his commands are one. If thou wilt not have Christ and his words, neither will he have thee nor thy words; but thou shalt ask in vain, thou shalt by-and-by give up asking, thou shalt become as a withered branch. Beloved, I am persuaded better things of you, and things that accompany salvation, though I thus speak.

Oh for grace to pass through these two-leaved gates, these two golden doors! "If ye abide in me, and my words abide in you." Push through the two, and enter into this large room—"Ye shall ask what ye will, and it shall be done unto you."

III. It is my last work to try to show WHY THIS PRIVILEGE SHOULD BE SO OBTAINED. This extraordinary power of prayer, why is it given to those who abide in Christ? May what I have to say encourage you to make the glorious attempt to win this pearl of great price! Why is it, that by abiding in Christ, and having his words abide in us, we get to this liberty and prevalence in prayer?

I answer, first, *because of the fulness of Christ.* You may very well ask what you will when you abide in Christ, because whatsoever you may require is already lodged in him. Good Bishop Hall worked out this thought in a famous passage. I will give you the substance of it. Do you desire the grace of the Spirit? Go to your Lord's anointing. Do you seek holiness? Go to his example. Do you desire pardon of sin? Look to his blood. Do you need mortification of sin? Look to his crucifixion. Do you need to be buried to the world? Go to his tomb. Do you want to feel the fulness of a heavenly life? Behold his resurrection. Would you rise above the world? Mark his ascension. Would you contemplate heavenly things? Remember his session at the right hand of God, and know that he "hath raised us up together, and made us sit together in heavenly places." I see clearly enough why the branch gets all it wants while it abides in the stem, since all it wants is already in the stem, and is placed there for the sake of the branch. What does the branch want more than the stem can give it? If it did want more it could not get it; for it has no other means of living but by sucking its life out of the stem. O my precious Lord, if I want anything which is not in thee, I desire always to be without it. I desire to be denied a wish which wanders outside of thyself. But if the supply of my desire is already in thee for me, why should I go elsewhere? Thou art my all; where else should I look? Beloved, "it pleased the Father that in him should all fulness dwell," and the good pleasure of the Father is our good pleasure also: we are glad to draw everything from Jesus. We feel sure that, ask what we will, we shall have it, since he has it ready for us.

The next reason for this is, *the richness of the Word of God.* Catch this thought, "If my words abide in you, ye shall ask what ye will, and it shall be done unto you." The best praying man is the man who is most believingly familiar with the promises of God. After all, prayer is nothing but taking God's promises to him, and saying to him, "Do as thou hast said." Prayer is the promise utilized. A prayer which is not based on a promise has no true foundation. If I go to the bank without a cheque I need not expect to get money; it is the "order to pay" which is my power inside the bank, and my warrant for expecting to receive. You that have Christ's words abiding in you are equipped with those things which the Lord regards with attention. If the Word of God abideth in you, you are the man that can pray, because you meet the great God with his own words, and thus overcome omnipotence with omnipotence. You put your finger down upon the very lines, and say, "Do as thou hast said." This is the best praying in all the world. O beloved, be filled with God's Word. Study what Jesus has said, what the Holy Ghost has left on record in this divinely-inspired Book, and in proportion as you feed on the Word, and are filled with the Word, and retain the Word in your faith, and obey the Word in your life—in that proportion you will be a master-man in the art of prayer. You have acquired skill as a wrestler with the covenant angel in proportion as you can plead the promises of your faithful God. Be well instructed in the doctrines of grace, and let the word of Christ dwell in you richly, that you may know how to prevail at the throne of grace. Abiding in Christ, and his words abiding in you, are like the right hand and the left hand of Moses, which were held up in prayer, so that Amalek was smitten, Israel was delivered, and God was glorified.

Let us go a little further: you still may say you do not quite see why a man who abides in Christ, and in whom Christ's words abide, should be allowed to ask whatever he wills, and it shall be done unto him. I answer you again: it is so, because *in such a man as that there is a predominance of grace which causes him to have a renewed will, which is according to the will of God.* Suppose a man of God is in prayer, and he thinks that such and such a thing is desirable, yet he remembers that he is nothing but a babe in the presence of his all-wise Father, and so he bows his will, and asks as a favour to be taught what to will. Though God bids him ask what he wills, he shrinks and cries, "My Lord, here is a request which I am not quite clear about. As far as I can judge, it is a desirable thing, and I will it; but, Lord, I am not fit to judge for myself, and therefore I pray thee, give not as I will, but as thou wilt." Do you not see that, when we are in such a condition as this, our real will is God's will. Deep down in our hearts we will only that which the Lord himself wills; and what is this but to ask what we will, and it is done to us? It becomes safe for God to say to the sanctified soul, "Ask what thou wilt, and it shall be done unto thee." The heavenly instincts of that man lead him right; the grace that is within his soul thrusts down all covetous lustings and foul desires, and his will is the actual shadow of God's will. The spiritual life is master in him, and so his aspirations are holy, heavenly, Godlike. He has been made a partaker of the divine nature; and as a son is like his father, so now in desire and will he is one with his God. As the echo answers to the voice, so does the renewed heart echo the mind of the Lord. Our desires are reflected beams of the divine will: ye shall ask what ye will, and it shall be even so.

You clearly see that the holy God cannot pick up a common man in the street, and say to him, "I will give you whatsoever you will." What would he ask for? He would ask for a good drink, or permission to enjoy himself in evil lust. It would be very unsafe to trust the most of men with this permit. But when the Lord has taken a man, and has new-made him, has quickened him into newness of life, and has formed him in the image of his dear Son, then he can trust him! Behold, the great Father treats us in our measure as he treats his Firstborn. Jesus could say, "I know that thou hearest me always"; and the Lord is educating us to the selfsame assurance. We can say with one of old, "My God will hear me." Do not your mouths water for this privilege of prevailing prayer? Do not your hearts long to get at this? It is by the way of holiness, it is by the way of union to Christ, it is by the way of a permanent abiding in him, and an obedient holding fast of his truth, that you are to come to this privilege. Behold the only safe and true way. When once that way is really trodden, it is a most sure and effectual way of gaining substantial power in prayer.

I have not quite done. A man will succeed in prayer *when his faith is strong;* and this is the case with those who abide in Jesus. It is faith that prevails in prayer. The real eloquence of prayer is a believing desire. "All things are possible to him that believeth." A man abiding in Christ with Christ's words abiding in him, is eminently a believer, and consequently eminently successful in prayer. He has strong faith indeed, for his faith has brought him into vital contact with Christ, and he is therefore at the source of every blessing, and may drink to his full at the well itself.

Such a man, once more, will also possess *the indwelling of the Spirit of God.* If we abide in Christ, and his words abide in us, then the Holy Ghost has come and taken up his residence in us; and what better help in prayer can we have? Is it not a wonderful thing that the Holy Ghost himself maketh intercession in the saints according to the will of God? He "maketh intercession for us with groanings that cannot be uttered." What man knoweth the mind of a man save the spirit of a man? The Spirit of God knows the mind of God, and he works in us to will what God wills, so that a believing man's prayer is God's purpose reflected in the soul as in a mirror. The eternal decrees of God project their shadows over the hearts of godly men in the form of prayer. What God intends to do he tells unto his servants by inclining them to ask him to do what he himself is resolved to do. God says, "I will do this and that"; but then he adds, "For this will I be enquired of by the house of Israel to do it for them." How clear it is that if we abide in Christ, and his words abide in us, we may ask what we will! For we shall only ask what the Spirit of God moves us to ask; and it were impossible that God the Holy Ghost and God the Father should be at cross-purposes with one another. What the one prompts us to ask, the other has assuredly determined to bestow.

I struck out a line just now to which I must return for a single moment. Beloved, do you not know that when we abide in Christ, and his words abide in us, the Father looks upon us with the same eye with which he looks upon his dear Son? Christ is the vine, and the vine includes the branches. The branches are a part of the vine. God, therefore, looks upon us as part of Christ—members of his body, of his flesh, and of his bones. Such is the Father's love to Jesus that he denies him nothing. He was obedient to death, even the death of the cross; therefore doth his Father love him, as the God-man Mediator, and he will grant him all his petitions. And is it so, that when you and I are in real union to Christ, the Lord God looks upon us in the same way as he looks on Jesus, and says to us, "I will deny you nothing; ye shall ask what ye will, and it shall be done unto you "? So do I understand the text.

I call your attention to the fact that in that fifteenth chapter, the ninth verse, which I did not read this morning, runs thus:—"As the Father hath loved me, so have I loved you." The same love which God gives to his Son, the Son gives to us; and therefore we are dwellers in the love of the Father and of the Son. How can our prayers be rejected? Will not infinite love have respect unto our petitions? O dear brother in Christ, if thy prayers speed not at the throne, suspect that there is some sin that hinders them: thy Father's love sees a necessity for chastening thee this way. If thou dost not abide in Christ, how canst thou hope to pray successfully? If thou dost pick and choose his words, and doubt this, and doubt that, how canst thou hope to speed at the throne? If thou art wilfully disobedient to any one of his words, will not this account for failure in prayer? But abide thou in Christ, and take fast hold upon his words, and be altogether his disciple, then shalt thou be heard of him. Sitting at Jesus' feet, hearing his words, thou mayest lift up thine eyes to his dear face, and say, "My Lord, hear me now"; and he will answer thee graciously: he will say unto thee, "I have heard thee in a time accepted, and in the day of salvation have I succoured thee. Ask what thou wilt, and it shall be done unto thee." Oh for power at the mercy-seat!

Beloved friends, do not hear this sermon, and then go away and forget it. Do try to reach this place of boundless influence. What a church we should be, if you were all mighty in prayer! Dear children of God, do you want to be half starved? Beloved brethren, do you desire to be poor, little, puny, drivelling children, who will never grow into men? I pray you, aspire to be strong in the Lord, and to enjoy this exceedingly high privilege. What an army would you be if you all had this power with God in prayer! It is within your reach, ye children of God! Only abide in Christ, and let his words abide in you, and then this special privilege will be yours. These are not irksome duties, but they are in themselves a joy. Go in for them with your whole heart, and then you shall get this added to you, that you shall ask what you will, and it shall be done unto you.

Unhappily, to a portion of this congregation my text says nothing at all; for some of you are not even in Christ, and therefore you cannot abide in him. O sirs, what shall I say to you? You seem to me to miss a very heaven even now. If there were no hell hereafter, it is hell enough not to know Christ now, not to know what it is to prevail with God in prayer, not to know the choice privilege of abiding in him, and his words abiding in you. Your first matter is that you believe in Jesus Christ to the saving of your souls, yielding your souls to his cleansing, your lives to his government. God hath sent him forth as a Saviour, accept him. Receive him as your Teacher; yield yourself up to him as your Master. May his gracious Spirit come and do this work upon you now; and then, after this, but not before, you may aspire to this honour. First of all—"Ye must be born again." I cannot say to you as you are now, "Grow," because you will only grow a bigger sinner. However much you may be developed, you will only develop what is in you: and that is, the heir of wrath will become more and more the child of evil. You must be made anew in Christ: there must be an absolute change, a reversal of all the currents of nature, a making you a new creature in Christ Jesus; and then you may aspire to abide in Christ, and let his words abide in you, and the consequent prevalence with God in prayer shall be yours.

Gracious Lord, help us. Poor creatures as we are, we can only lie at thy feet. Come thyself, and uplift us to thyself, for thy mercy's sake! Amen.

3
COMFORT FOR THOSE WHOSE PRAYERS ARE FEEBLE

"Hide not thine ear at my breathing." Lamentations 3:56

"The Lord hears the poor, and the ignorant, and the needy; he loves to hear their cry."

~

YOUNG beginners in grace are very apt to compare themselves with advanced disciples, and so to become discouraged; and tried saints fall into the like habit. They see those of God's people who are upon the mount, enjoying the light of their Redeemer's countenance, and, comparing their own condition with the joy of the saints, they write bitter things against themselves, and conclude that surely they are not the people of God. This course is as foolish as though the lambs should suspect themselves not to be of the flock because they are not sheep, or as though a sick man should doubt his existence because he is not able to walk or run as a man in good health. But since this evil habit is very common, it is our duty to seek after the dispirited and cast-down ones, and comfort them. That is our errand in this short discourse. We hear the Master's words, "Comfort ye, comfort ye my people," and we will endeavour to obey them by his Spirit's help.

Upon the matter of prayer, many are dispirited because they cannot yet pray as advanced believers do, or because, during some peculiar crisis of their spiritual history, their prayers do not appear to them to be so fervent and acceptable as is the case with other Christians. Perhaps God may have a message to some troubled ones in the present address, and may the Holy Ghost apply it with power to such!

"Hide not thine ear at my breathing." This is a singular description of prayer, is it not? Frequently, prayer is said to have a voice; it is so in this verse: "Thou hast heard my voice." Prayer has a melodious voice in the ear of our Heavenly Father. Frequently, too, prayer is expressed by a cry. It is so in this verse: "Hide not thine ear at my cry." A cry is the natural, plaintive utterance of sorrow, and has as much power to move the heart of God as a babe's cry to touch a mother's tenderness. But there are times when we cannot speak with the voice, nor even cry, and then a prayer may be expressed by a moan, or a groan, or a tear,—"the heaving of a sigh, the falling of a tear." But, possibly, we may not even get so far as that, and may have to say, like one of old, "Like a crane or a swallow, so do I chatter." Our prayer, as heard by others, may be a kind of irrational utterance. We may feel as if we moaned like wounded beasts, rather than prayed like intelligent men; and we may even fall below that, for, in the text, we have a kind of prayer which is less than a moan or a sigh. It is called a *breathing:* "Hide not thine ear at my breathing." The man is too far gone for a glance of the eye, or the moaning of the heart, he scarcely breathes, but that faint breath is prayer. Though unuttered and unexpressed by any sounds which could reach a human ear, yet God hears the breathing of his servant's soul, and hides not his ear from it.

We shall teach three or four lessons from the present use of the expression "breathing."

I. WHEN WE CANNOT PRAY AS WE WOULD, IT IS GOOD TO PRAY AS WE CAN.

Bodily weakness should never be urged by us as a reason for ceasing to pray; in fact, no living child of God will ever think of such a thing. If I cannot bend the knees of my body because I am so weak, my prayers from my bed shall be on *their* knees, my heart shall be on its knees, and pray as acceptably as aforetime. Instead of relaxing prayer because the body suffers, true hearts, at such times, usually double their petitions. Like Hezekiah, they turn their face to the wall that they may see no earthly object, and then they look at the things invisible, and talk with the Most High, ay, and often in a sweeter and more familiar manner than they did in the days of their health and strength. If we are so faint that we can only lie still and breathe, let every breath be prayer.

Nor should a true Christian relax his prayer through *mental difficulties*, I mean those perturbations which distract the mind, and prevent the concentration of our thoughts. Such ills will happen to us. Some of us are often much depressed, and are frequently so tossed to and fro in mind that, if prayer were an operation which required the faculties to be all at their best, as in the working of abstruse mathematical problems, we should not at such times be able to pray at all. But, brethren, when the mind is very heavy, then is not the time to give up praying, but rather to redouble our supplications. Our blessed Lord and Master was driven by distress of mind into the most sad condition; he said, "My soul is exceeding sorrowful, even unto death;" yet he did not for that reason say, "I cannot pray;" but, on the contrary, he sought the well-known shades of the olive grove, and there unburdened his heavy heart, and poured out his soul like water before the Lord. Never let us consider ourselves to be too ill or too distracted to pray. A Christian ought never to be in such a state of mind that he feels bound to say, "I do not feel that I could pray;" or, if he does, let him pray till he feels he can pray. Not to pray because you do not feel fit to pray is like saying, "I will not take medicine because I am too ill." Pray for prayer: pray yourself, by the Spirit's assistance, into a praying frame. It is good to strike when the iron is hot, but some make cold iron hot by striking. We have sometimes eaten till we have gained an appetite, so let us pray till we pray. God will help you in the pursuit of duty, not in the neglect of it.

The same is the case with regard to *spiritual sicknesses*. Sometimes it is not merely the body or the mind which is affected, but our inner nature is dull, stupid, lethargic, so that, when it is time for prayer, we do not feel the spirit of prayer. Moreover, perhaps our faith is flagging, and how shall we pray when faith is so weak? Possibly we are suspicious as to whether we are the people of God at all, and we are molested by the recollection of our shortcomings. Now the tempter will whisper, "Do not pray just now; your heart is not in a fit condition for it." My dear brother, you will not become fit for prayer by keeping away from the mercy-seat, but to lie groaning or breathing at its foot is the best preparation for pleading before the Lord. We are not to aim at a self-wrought preparation of our hearts that we may come to God aright, but "the preparations of the heart in man, and the answer of the tongue, are from the Lord." If I feel myself disinclined to pray, then is the time when I need to pray more than ever. Possibly, when the soul leaps and exults in communion with God, it might more safely refrain from prayer than at those seasons when it drags heavily in devotion. Alas! my Lord, does my soul go wandering away from thee? Then, come back my heart, I will drag thee back by force of grace, I will not cease to cry till the Spirit of God has made thee return to thine allegiance. What, my Christian brother, because thou feelest idle, is that a reason why thou shouldst stay thine hand, and not serve thy God? Nay, but away with thine idleness, and resolutely bend thy soul to service. So, under a sense of prayerlessness, be more intent on prayer. Repent that thou canst not repent, groan that thou canst not groan, and pray until thou dost pray; in so doing God will help thee.

But, it may be objected, that *sometimes we are placed in great difficulty as to circumstances*, so that we may be excused from prayer. Brethren, there are no circumstances in which we should cease to pray in some form of other. "But I have so many cares." Who among us has not? If we are never to pray till all our cares are over, surely then we shall either never pray at all, or pray when we have no more need for it. What did Abram do when he offered sacrifice to God? When the patriarch had slaughtered the appointed creatures, and laid them on the altar, certain vultures and kites came hovering around, ready to pounce upon the consecrated flesh. What did the patriarch do then? "When the fowls came down upon the carcases, Abram drove them away."* So must we ask for grace to drive our cares away from our devotions. That was a wise direction which the prophet gave to the poor woman when the Lord was about to multiply her oil. "Go, take the cruse," he said, "pour out the oil, and fill the borrowed vessels;" but what did he also say? "Shut the door upon thee." If the door had been open, some of her gossiping neighbours would have looked in, and said, "What are you doing? Do you really hope to fill all these jars out of that little oil cruse? Why, woman, you must be mad!" I am afraid she would not have been able to perform that act of faith if the objectors had not been shut out. It is a grand thing when the soul can bolt the doors against distractions, and keep out those intruders; for then it is that prayer and faith will perform their miracle, and our soul shall be filled with the blessing of the Lord. Oh, for grace to overcome circumstances, and, at least to breathe out prayer, if we cannot reach to a more powerful form of it!

Perhaps, however, you declare that your circumstances are more difficult than I can imagine, for *you are surrounded by those who mock you, and, besides, Satan himself molests you.* Ah! then, dear brother or sister, under such circumstances, instead of restraining prayer, be ten times more diligent. Your position is pre-eminently perilous, you cannot afford to live away from the throne of grace, do not therefore attempt it. As to threatened persecution, pray in defiance of it. Remember how Daniel opened his window, and prayed to his God as he had done aforetime. Let the God of Daniel be your God in the chamber of prayer, and he will be your God in the lions' den. As for the devil, be sure that nothing will drive him away like prayer. That couplet is correct which declares that—

> "Satan trembles when he sees
> The Weakest saint upon his knees."

Whatever thy position, if thou canst not speak, cry; if thou canst not cry, groan; if thou canst not groan, let there be "groanings which cannot be uttered;" and if thou canst not even rise to that point, let thy prayer be at least a breathing,—a vital, sincere desire, the outpouring of thine inner life in the simplest and weakest form, and God will accept it. In a word, when you cannot pray as you would, take care to pray as you can.

II. But now, a second word of instruction. It is clear from the text, from many other passages of Scripture, and from general observation, that THE BEST OF MEN HAVE USUALLY FOUND THE GREATEST FAULT WITH THEIR OWN PRAYERS.

This arises from the fact that they present living prayers in real earnest, and feel far more than they can express. A mere formalist can always pray so as to please himself. What has he to do but to open his book, and read the prescribed words, or bow his knee, and repeat such phrases as suggest themselves to his memory or his fancy? Like the Tartarian Praying Machine, give but the wind and the wheel, and the business is fully arranged. So much knee-bending and talking, and the prayer is done. The formalist's prayers are always good, or, rather, always bad, alike. But the living child of God never offers a prayer which pleases himself; his standard is above his attainments; he wonders that God listens to him, and though he knows he will be heard for Christ's sake, yet he accounts it a wonderful instance of condescending mercy that such poor prayers as his should ever reach the ears of the Lord God of Sabaoth.

If it be asked in what respect holy men find fault with their prayers, we reply, that *they complain of the narrowness of their desires.* O God, thou hast bidden me open my mouth wide, and thou wilt fill it, but I do not open my mouth! Thou art ready to bestow great things upon me, but I am not ready to receive great things. I am straitened, but it is not in thee; I am straitened in my own desires. Dear brethren, when we read of Hugh Latimer on his knees perpetually crying out, "O God, give back the gospel to England," and sometimes praying so long that he could not rise, being an aged man, and they had to lift him up from the prison-floor, and he would still keep on crying, "O God, give back the gospel to poor England," we may well wonder that some of us do not pray in the same way. The times are as bad as Latimer's, and we have as great need to pray as he had, "O God, drive away this Popery once again, and give back the gospel to England." Then, think of John Knox. Why, that man's prayers were like great armies for power, and he would wrestle all night with God that he would kindle the light of the gospel in Scotland. He averred that he had gained his desire, and I believe he had, and that the light which burns so brightly in Scotland is much to be attributed to that man's supplications. We do not pray like these men; we have no heart to ask for great things. A revival is waiting, the cloud is hovering over England, and we do not know how to bring it down. Oh, that God may find some true spirits who shall be as conductors to bring down the fire divine! We want it much, but our poor breathings—they do not come to much more,—have no force, no expansiveness, no great-heartedness, no prevalence in them.

Then, how far we fail in the matter of *faith!* We do not pray as if we believed. Believing prayer is a grasping and a wrestling, but ours is a mere puffing and blowing, a little breathing,—not much more. God is true, and we pray to him as if he were false. He means what he says, and we treat his Word as if it were spoken in jest. The master-fault of our prayer is want of faith.

How often do we lack *earnestness!* Such men as Luther had their will of heaven because they *would* have it. God's Spirit made them resolute in intercession, and they would not come away from the mercy-seat till their suit was granted; but we are cold, and consequently feeble, and our poor, poor prayers, in the prayer-meeting, in the closet, and at the family altar, languish and almost die.

How much, alas, is there of *impurity of motive* to mar our prayers! We ask for revival, but we want our own church to get the blessing, that we may have the credit of it. We pray God to bless our work, and it is because we wish to hear men say what good workers we are. The prayer is good in itself, but our smutty fingers spoil it. Oh, that we could offer supplication as it should be offered! Blessed be God, there is One who can wash our prayers for us; but, truly, our very tears need to be wept over, and our prayers want praying over again. The best thing we ever do needs to be washed in the fountain filled with blood, or God can only look upon it as a sin.

Another fault good men see in their supplications is this, that *they stand at such a distance from God in praying*, they do not draw near enough to him. Are not some of you oppressed with a sense of the distance there is between you and God? You know there is a God, and you believe he will answer you; but it is not always that you come right up to him, even to his feet, and, as it were, lay hold upon him, and say, "O my Father, hearken to the voice of thy chosen, and let the cry of the blood of thy Son come up before thee!" Oh, for prayers which enter within the veil, and approach to the mercy-seat! Oh, for petitioners who are familiar with the cherubim, and the brightness which shines between their wings! May God help us to pray better! But this I feel sure of,—you who plead most prevalently are just those who will think the least of your own prayers, and be most grateful to God that he deigns to listen to you, and most anxious that he would help you to pray after a nobler sort.

III. A third lesson is this,—THE POWER OF PRAYER IS NOT TO BE MEASURED BY ITS OUTWARD EXPRESSION.

A breathing is a prayer from which God does not hide his ear. It is a great truth undoubtedly, and full of much comfort too, that our prayers are not powerful in proportion to their expression; for, if so, the Pharisee would have succeeded, since he evidently had greater gifts than the Publican had. I have no doubt, if there had been a regular prayer-meeting, and the Pharisee and the Publican had attended, we should have called on the Pharisee to pray. I do not think the people of God would have enjoyed his prayer, nor have felt any kinship of spirit with him; and yet, very naturally, on account of his gifts, he would have taken upon himself to engage in public devotion; or, if that Pharisee would not have done so, I have heard of other Pharisees who would. No doubt the man's spirit was bad, but then his expression was good. He could put his oration so neatly, and pour it out so accurately Let all men know that God does not care for that. The sigh of the Publican reached his ear, and won the blessing but the boastful phrases of the Pharisee were an abomination unto him.

If our prayers were forcible according to their expression, then rhetoric would be more valuable than grace, and a scholastic education would be better than sanctification; but it is not so. Some of us may be able to express ourselves very fluently from the force of natural gifts, but it should always be to us an anxious question whether our prayer is a prayer which God will receive; for we ought to know, and must know by this time, that we often pray best when we stammer and stutter, and we pray worst when words come rolling like a torrent, one after another. God is not moved by words; they are but a noise to him. He is only moved by the deep thought and the heaving emotion which dwell in the innermost spirit. It were a sorry business for you, who are poor, if God only heard us according to the beauty of our utterances; for it may be that your education was so neglected that there is no hope of your ever being able to speak grammatically; and, besides, it may be, from your limited information, that you could not use the phrases which sound so well. But the Lord hears the poor, and the ignorant, and the needy; he loves to hear their cry. What cares he for the grammar of the prayer? It is the soul of it that he wants; and if you cannot string three words of the Queen's English together correctly, yet, if your soul can breathe itself out before the Most High anyhow, if it be but warm, hearty, sincere, earnest petitioning, there is power in your prayer, and none the less power in it because of its broken words, nor would it be an advantage to you, so far as the Lord is concerned, if those words were not broken, but were well composed. Ought not this to comfort us, then?

Even if we are gifted with facility of expression, we sometimes find that our power of utterance fails us. Under very heavy grief, a man cannot speak as he was wont to do. Circumstances can make the most eloquent tongue grow slow of speech; it matters not, your prayer is as good as it was before. You call upon God in public, and you sit down, and think that your confused prayer was of no service to the church. You know not in what scales God weighs your prayer; not by quantity, but by quality, not by the outward dress of verbiage, but by the inner soul and the intense earnestness that was in it does he compute its value. Do you not sometimes rise from your knees in your little room, and say, "I do not think I have prayed, I could not feel at home in prayer"? Nine times out of every ten, those prayers are most prevalent with God which we think are the least acceptable; but when we glory in our prayer, God will have nothing to do with it. If you see any beauty in your own supplication, God will not; for you have evidently been looking at your prayer, and not at him. But when your soul sees so much *his* glory that she cries, "How shall I speak unto thee,—I who am but dust and ashes?" when she sees so much his goodness that she is hampered in expression by the depth of her own humiliation, oh, then it is that your prayer is best. There may be more prayer in a groan than in an entire liturgy; there may be more acceptable devotion in a tear that damps the floor of yonder pew than in all the hymns we have sung, or in all the supplications which we have uttered. It is not the outward, it is the inward; it is not the lips, it is the heart which the Lord regards; if you can only breathe, still your prayer is accepted by the Most High.

I desire that this truth may come home to any one of you who says, "I cannot pray." It is not true. If it were necessary that, in order to pray, you should talk for a quarter of an hour together, or that you should say pretty things, why then I would admit that you could not pray; but if it is only to say from your heart, "God be merciful to me a sinner;" ay, and if prayer is not saying anything at all, but desiring, longing, hoping for mercy, for pardon, for salvation, no man may say, "I cannot," unless he is honest enough to add, "I cannot because I will not; I love my sins too well, and have no faith in Christ; I do not desire to be saved." If you will to pray, O my hearer, you can pray! He who gives the will joins the ability to it.

And oh! let me say, do not sleep this night until you have tried and proved the power of prayer. If you feel a burden on your heart, tell the Lord of it. Cover your face, and speak with him. Even that you need not do, for I suppose that Hannah did not cover her face when Eli saw her lips move, and supposed that she was drunken. Nay, your lips need not even move; your soul can now say, "Save me, my God, convince me of sin, lead me to the cross; save me to-night; let me not end another day as thine enemy; let me not go into the cares of another week unabsolved, with thy wrath hanging over me like a thunder-cloud! Save me, save me, O my God!" Such prayers, though utterly wordless, shall not be powerless, but shall be heard in heaven.

IV. We will close with a fourth practical lesson,— FEEBLE PRAYERS ARE HEARD IN HEAVEN.

Why is it that feeble prayers are understood of God and heard in heaven? There are three reasons.

First, *the feeblest prayer, if it be sincere, is written by the Holy Spirit upon the heart, and God will always own the handwriting of the Holy Spirit.* Frequently, certain kind friends from Scotland send me for the Orphanage some portions of what one of them called the other day "filthy lucre,"—namely, dirty £1 notes. Now these £1 notes certainly look as if they were of small value. Still, they bear the proper signature, and they pass well enough, and I am very grateful for them. Many a prayer that is written on the heart by the Holy Spirit seems written with faint ink, and, moreover, it appears to be blotted and defiled by our imperfection; but the Holy Spirit can always read his own handwriting. He knows his own notes; and when he has issued a prayer, he will not disown it. Therefore, the breathing which the Holy Ghost works in us will be acceptable with God.

Moreover, *God, our ever-blessed Father, has a quick ear to hear the breathing of any of his children.* When a mother has a sick child, it is marvellous how quick her ears become while attending it. Good woman, we wonder she does not fall asleep. If you hired a nurse, it is ten to one *she* would. But the dear child, in the middle of the night, does not need to cry for water, or even speak; there is a little quick breathing,—who will hear it? No one would except the mother; but her ears are quick, for they are in her child's heart. So, if there is a heart in the world that longs for God, God's ear is already in that poor sinner's heart. He will hear it. There is not a good desire on earth but the Lord has heard it. I recollect when, at one time, I was a little afraid to preach the gospel to sinners as sinners, and yet I wanted to do so, so I used to say, "If you have but a millionth part of a desire, come to Christ." I dare say more than that now; but, at the same time, I will say that at once,—if you have a millionth part of a desire, if you have only a little breathing,—if you desire to be reconciled, if you desire to be pardoned, if you would be forgiven, if there is only half a good thought formed in your soul, do not check it, do not stifle it, and do not think that God will reject it.

And, then, there is another reason, namely, that *the Lord Jesus Christ is always ready to take the most imperfect prayer, and perfect it for us.* If our prayers had to go up to heaven as they are, they would never succeed; but they find a Friend on the way, and therefore they prosper. A poor person has a petition to be sent in to some government personage, and if he had to write it himself, it would puzzle all the officers in Downing-street to make out what he meant; but he is wise enough to find out a friend who can write, or he comes round to his minister, and says, "Sir, will you make this petition right for me? Will you put it into good English, so that it can be presented?" And then the petition goes in a very different form. Even thus, the Lord Jesus Christ takes our poor prayers, fashions them over again, and presents the petition with the addition of his own signature, and the Lord sends us answers of peace.

The feeblest prayer in the world is heard when it has Christ's seal to it. I mean, he puts his precious blood upon it; and wherever God sees the blood of Jesus, he must and will accept the desire which it endorses. Go thou to Jesus, sinner, even if thou canst not pray, and let the breathing of thy soul be, "Be merciful to me, wash me, cleanse me, save me," and it shall be done; for God will not hear your prayer so much as hear his Son's blood, "which speaketh better things than that of Abel." A louder voice than yours shall prevail for you, and your feeble breathings shall come up to God covered over with the omnipotent pleadings of the great High Priest who never asks in vain.

I have been aiming thus to comfort those distressed ones who say they cannot pray; but, ere I close, I must add, how inexcusable are those who, knowing all this, continue prayerless, Godless, and Christless! If there were no mercy to be had, you could not be blamed for not having it. If there were no Saviour for sinners, a sinner might be excused for remaining in his sin. But there is a fountain, and it is open; why then wash ye not in it? Mercy is to be had "without money and without price,"—it is to be had by asking for it. Sometimes poor men are shut up in the condemned cell, sentenced to be hanged; but suppose they could have a free pardon by asking for it, and they did not do so, who would pity them? God will give his blessing to everyone who is moved to seek for it sincerely at his hands on this one sole and only condition,—that that soul will trust in Jesus; and even that is not a condition, for he gives repentance and faith, and enables sinners to believe in his dear Son. Behold Christ crucified, the saddest and yet the gladdest sight the sun ever beheld! Behold the eternal Son of God made flesh, and bleeding out his life! A surpassing marvel of woe and love! A look at him will save you. Though ye are on the borders of the grave, and on the brink of hell, by one look at Jesus crucified your guilt shall be cancelled, your debts for ever discharged before the throne of God, and yourselves led into joy and peace. Oh, that you would give that look! Breathe the prayer, "Lord, give me the faith of thine elect, and save me with a great salvation!" Though it be only a breathing, yet, as the old Puritan says, when God feels the breath of his child upon his face, he smiles; and he will feel your breath, and smile on you, and bless you. May he do so, for his name's sake! Amen.

4

BOLDNESS AT THE THRONE

"Let us therefore come boldly unto the throne of grace."—
Hebrews 4:16

"The very invitation to us to pray implies that there are blessings waiting for us at the mercy-seat: "let us therefore come boldly unto the throne of grace."

~

PRAYER occupies a most important place in the life of the Christian. "Behold, he prayeth," was one of the first and also one of the surest indications of the conversion of Saul of Tarsus. No one begins to live the life of faith who has not also begun to pray, and as prayer is needful at the commencement of the Christian career, so is it needful all through. A Christian's vigour, happiness, growth, and usefulness all depend upon prayer. It is—

> "His watchword at the gates of death,
> He enters heaven with prayer."

I suppose that, even there, we shall continue to pray. At all events, we read of the souls under the altar crying with a loud voice, and saying, "How long, O Lord, holy and true, dost thou not judge and avenge our blood on them that dwell on the earth?" I imagine that, in heaven, we shall still lift up our hearts in prayer for the spread of Christ's kingdom, though our principal occupation there will be that of praise. But prayer is always needed here; every day, every hour, every moment we have cause for crying unto the Most High.

> "Long as they live should Christians pray,"

for only while they pray do they truly live.

It is because of the supreme importance of prayer that we find so much about it in the Scriptures. The Holy Ghost continually encourages us to pray, by precept, and promise, and example; and one conspicuous instance of that encouragement is the exhortation we are now to consider: "Let us therefore come boldly unto the throne of grace."

So, coming at once to the text, notice that we have here, first, *a description of our great resort for prayer:* "the throne of grace." Secondly, we have *a loving exhortation:* "let us come unto the throne of grace." Thirdly, we have *a qualifying adverb*, telling us how we are to come: "let us come boldly." Fourthly, we have *a reason given for boldness.* The reason is in the context; we shall also think of other reasons, and then shall close with *the* reason upon which Paul laid the stress of the argument in writing to the Hebrews: "let us therefore come boldly unto the throne of grace."

I. First, then, dear friends, we have A DESCRIPTION OF OUR GREAT RESORT FOR PRAYER: "the throne of grace."

Under the law, there was to be an ark overlaid within and without with pure gold, and above the ark was to be the mercy-seat of pure gold, with the golden cherubim covering the mercy-seat with their wings. This mysterious emblem no one ever saw except the high priest, and he saw it only once a year, and then but dimly, for he saw it through the smoke of the incense which he presented before the Lord. It was a secret thing, but now it is revealed to us, for the veil has been rent, and the symbol taken away, that we may now come boldly right up to the throne of the heavenly grace.

I was conversing, some time ago, with a member of the Catholic and Apostolic Church, who took great pains to instruct me as to the meaning of the various offices and ordinances of the body with which he was connected. After he had explained a great many mysteries, to his own satisfaction, if not to my edification, he pointed out the position of the saints at the present day, and then I felt that it was time to answer him, so I said, "I do not believe that Christians are intended to go crawling about the outer court, and keeping far off from the holy place, for the apostle Paul says, 'Let us therefore come boldly unto the throne of grace,' right into the holy of holies, for there is no longer any separating veil to keep us away from the mercy-seat. As a believer in the Lord Jesus Christ, my place is not in the outer court, nor even in the court of the priests; I have advanced beyond them, and come right up to the throne of grace, that I may there obtain mercy, and find grace to help in time of need." That is the position of all true Christians, not only on one day of the year, but every day.

I wish that all believers could realize the privileges to which they were born when they were created anew in Christ Jesus. You may have heard a whole congregation saying, "Lord, have mercy upon us, and incline our hearts to keep this law," and you may have seen them all shivering there at the foot of Sinai, with the lightning flashing above them, and the thunder pealing around them. Yet it is possible that at least some of them may have had the right to come before the Lord as his own dear children through faith in Jesus Christ; and if so, they might have said to him, "Lord, thou hast had mercy upon us, thou hast blotted out all our transgressions; and now we are not under the law, but under grace, and are completely delivered from the thraldom of the old covenant of works, and are put under the new covenant of grace, that we may serve thee in newness of spirit, and not in the oldness of the letter." Blessed are they who are enjoying the liberty wherewith Christ makes his people free, and who therefore come boldly right up to the throne of grace.

The mercy-seat, then, is where the high priest typically came once in the year, and our great High Priest, "by his own blood entered in once into the holy place, having obtained eternal redemption for us." As he died, he tore down the separating veil, and threw the holiest of all open to all who believe in him, and he hath made them kings and priests unto God, so that where the high priest stood is where they stand in Christ Jesus. That place is so solemn and awe-inspiring that we might fear and quake at the very thought of coming to it were it not for this and other similar exhortations, "Let us therefore come boldly unto the throne of grace, that we may obtain mercy, and find grace to help in time of need."

Our mercy-seat is called "a throne" because *we come there to God as a King*, and we, by faith, behold him in his excellent glory and majesty. He is our Father, and our Friend, but he is also "the King eternal, immortal, invisible," so we approach even the throne of grace with the deepest awe and reverence. We come to this throne with the utmost confidence, for God gives as a King, and therefore we ask largely and expectantly. John Newton caught the very spirit of this verse when he wrote,—

> "Thou art coming to a King,
> Large petitions with thee bring;
> For his grace and power are such,
> None can ever ask too much."

It is a throne of grace, where no ordinary monarch presides, but where One is sitting who is infinite and all-sufficient, One who can bestow upon us more than we ask, or ever think of asking, and yet not impoverish himself in the slightest degree. Do you always remember, beloved, in coming to the mercy-seat, that you are coming to a King, and to One who gives like a King? Do you always open your mouth wide, and ask great things of the King who is so ready to bestow them upon you?

In drawing near to God in prayer, *we come to a King who sits upon a throne of grace*. That word "grace" is one of the choicest in the whole description of our great resort for prayer. We might well have trembled if we had been bidden to come to a throne of justice; we might have been afraid to come to a throne of power alone; but we need not hesitate to come to the throne of grace, where God sits on purpose to dispense grace. It would be terrible if we had to pray to a just God if he was not also a Saviour; if we could only see the awful glare of Sinai without the blessed attractions of the atonement made on Calvary. If we can see the "rainbow round about the throne, in sight like unto an emerald," the token of God's covenant love and grace, then we can pray very differently from the way in which we should pray if we could only see the naked sword of divine justice brandished to and fro to keep us back from the holy God who would not have his peerless majesty polluted by our sinful presence. Let us ever remember that, when we pray aright, we deal with God on terms of grace, and answers to our petitions come to us, not according to our deservings, but according to his infinite mercy and grace in Christ Jesus our Lord.

It is also very comforting to us to observe that *the God who hears prayer is enthroned and glorified*. The God of grace sits upon the throne of grace, and so grace reigns supreme at the place where God meets with us in prayer. The hand of grace is full of blessings through the atoning sacrifice of Jesus Christ, and that hand is happily employed in dispensing royal largess among the poverty-stricken sons and daughters of men. Come hither then, all ye who feel your need of grace; be not afraid to approach the throne of grace. Since Jesus Christ has taken upon himself our nature, and suffered in our stead, the throne to which the sinner is bidden to draw nigh is a throne of superlative, unlimited, reigning grace;—grace that pardons, grace that regenerates, grace that adopts, grace that preserves, grace that sanctifies, grace that perfects, and makes meet for glory. Happy is the preacher whose privilege it is to invite sinners to come to such a blessed meeting-place with God, but happier far will be the sinners who shall have the grace to come to that meeting-place! May many here be among them!

II. Now, secondly, we have A LOVING EXHORTATION: "let us come unto the throne of grace."

Who is it that gives this exhortation? Why did he put it in this form? We might have expected the exhortation to be simply, "Come boldly unto the throne of grace;" or even "Go boldly unto the throne of grace;" but it is put in the form of an invitation from someone who urges us to go with him; who is this?

Well, first, it is *from Paul, who had himself proved the power of prayer.* "Paul? Have I not heard his name before?" Oh, yes! "But had he not once another name?" Yes, his name was Saul. "Then, surely, that must have been the man who persecuted the saints of God, who was exceedingly mad against them, and against the Christ whom they loved more than they loved their own lives." Yes, that is the man, only he has been so changed by grace that he is a new man in Christ Jesus; and now he confesses that he was the chief of the sinners whom Jesus came to save. It is this saved sinner who is now a saint of God, and an apostle of Jesus Christ, who writes to his fellow-believers, "Let us therefore come boldly unto the throne of grace." Methinks that I can summon up courage to go to the mercy-seat in such company as this. If the chief of sinners is going to the throne of grace, I also may go. I may be the chief of sinners too under another aspect; and if so, there will be a pair of us, and we will go together.

Yes, it was Paul who gave this exhortation, a man of like passions with ourselves, who was once as great a sinner as any of us have ever been; he puts out his hand to us, and he says, "Come along, brothers and sisters; let us come boldly unto the throne of grace." When he gave this exhortation, Paul had become an experienced believer who had often gone to the throne of grace, and there proved the power of prayer. He was no stranger at the mercy-seat, he had done much heavenly business with his Master there; so now, having proved the power of prayer, he does not speak as a mere theorist, but as a practical man, who had put the matter to the test, and therefore knew that God answered prayer. So he wrote to those who had not had such a wonderful experience as his had been, to those whose knowledge of divine things was far inferior to his own, and linking himself with them he said, "Let us come boldly unto the throne of grace."

It always does me good to hear an aged Christian talk about the Lord Jesus Christ. I recollect, at this moment, a venerable minister who has long gone to glory. I heard him make almost his dying speech. He had been blind for many years; and when he rose at the communion table, and told us of the lovingkindness of the Lord toward him, and of how he had tried and tested his God in the deep waters of affliction, and had always found him faithful; and when he bade us, young people, be sure to put our trust in the Lord, for he was well worth trusting, he did us all good. I think it is in some such way as this that the apostle Paul, a man of deep and varied experience, writes to the Hebrews, and through them to us also, and says, as one who has tried and proved the power of prayer, "Let us therefore come boldly unto the throne of grace."

It is, however, not only Paul who speaks in this exhortation; but it seems to me that *this exhortation comes, through Paul, from the whole Church of Christ.* Paul was a representative man, and as he penned these lines it seems as though the entire Church of God was speaking through his words. Even the saints in glory appear to cry out to us, "Come ye boldly to the throne of grace; we can urge you to do so from a recollection of our own experience, for we long ago tried and proved the efficacy of prayer in every emergency that we had to face." It is certain that all the saints on earth unite in this exhortation, "Let us therefore come boldly unto the throne of grace." From many a sick bed, where aged Christians have been for years pining away,—nay, I correct myself, and say, where they have been melting into glory as the morning star melts into the sunlight,—from many such a bed, where faith has triumphed over physical weakness and pain, I hear the cry, "Let us come boldly unto the throne of grace." From many a night-watcher, compelled by terrible pain to lie awake, and guard the night with prayer, as the sentinels of the Church of God, I hear the cry, "Let us come boldly unto the throne of grace." From many another child of God, who, in the midst of activities and trials combined, has daily and hourly to draw his strength from the Most High by fervent supplication, I hear the cry, "Let us come boldly unto the throne of grace." And from many who, through prayer, have been enabled to do great exploits in the name of Jesus, having cast themselves by faith upon a prayer-hearing and prayer-answering God, and who are to-day the living evidences of what divine grace can accomplish through human instrumentality,—from these also I hear the cry, "Let us come boldly unto the throne of grace." The church militant, with its blood-red banner floating in the breeze, marches bravely on to the conflict, crying, "Let us come boldly unto the throne of grace, that we may obtain mercy, and find grace to help in time of need."

But I hear also, in this exhortation, a voice much more powerful than that of the apostle Paul, or even of the whole Church of Christ, for it seems to me to come *from the Holy Spirit himself*, for Paul wrote as he was moved by the Holy Ghost. I think I am not going too far when I say that the Divine Spirit, who dwells in all the saints, is now speaking through the inspired page, and saying to us, "Let us come boldly unto the throne of grace." Paul wrote to the Romans, "We know not what we should pray for as we ought: but the Spirit itself maketh intercession for us with groanings which cannot be uttered. And he that searcheth the hearts knoweth what is the mind of the Spirit, because he maketh intercession for the saints according to the will of God." It appears to me that, in our text, the Spirit, speaking in the soft and gentle accents that the Comforter delights to use, is not so much bidding us go to the throne of grace, as promising that he will go there with us; and, surely, we will go if he will accompany us. As it is his divine voice that says, "Let us come boldly unto the throne of grace," let us obey the gracious exhortation. This is not the only time that the Spirit and the Church of Christ say the same thing, for we read, in the Revelation, "The Spirit and the bride say, Come;" so, here, the Spirit and the bride both seem to me to say,

"Let us come boldly unto the throne of grace." Therefore, all ye who form part of the mystical bride of Christ, hear the Spirit's gentle call, comply with his exhortation, and come boldly unto the throne of grace.

III. Now, thirdly, we have A QUALIFYING ADVERB: "let us come *boldly* unto the throne of grace."

We must not mistake the meaning of this word "boldly." Paul does not say, "Let us come proudly unto the throne of grace." God forbid that we should do that. Abraham's prayer for Sodom and Gomorrah is an admirable model of how we are to come boldly unto the throne of grace; for, although he pleaded again and again for the guilty cities of the plain, he said, "Behold now, I have taken upon me to speak unto the Lord, which am but dust and ashes." The greatest boldness in prayer is perfectly consistent with the lowest self-humiliation.

Neither must we ever think of coming before the Lord arrogantly or presumptuously, for it is to a "throne" that we are bidden to come, although that throne is "the throne of grace." I have heard prayers that have seemed to me like dictating to God, rather than the humble, reverent petitions which should be presented by the creature to the Creator, or by the children of God to their loving Father in heaven. We are to come boldly unto the throne of grace, yet always with submission in our hearts, even as our Lord himself prayed, "Nevertheless not as I will, but as thou wilt."

I think that, by this adverb "boldly" is meant that *we may come constantly*, at all times. Eastern potentates would only admit petitioners to their presence just when they pleased. Though Esther was made queen by Ahasuerus, she was not allowed to go near him unless she was specially called; but it is not so with us. The path to the throne of grace is always open, there are no guards to bar the way of those who come in the right spirit. There are no set times for prayer; one hour is as good as any other for coming to the throne of grace. Whenever the Spirit of God inclines the heart to pray, the ear of God is open to hear our supplications, and the mouth of God is open to grant us gracious answers of peace.

"Boldly" also means that *we may come unreservedly*, with all sorts of petitions. Whatever it is that lies as a burden upon thine heart, come with it to the throne of grace. Dost thou really need some great thing? Then, come and ask for it. Or dost thou need some little thing? Then, come and ask for it. Hast thou some care that is crushing thee into the very dust? Come and leave it at the mercy-seat. Hast thou some little care that worries thee, some thorn in the flesh, some messenger from Satan to buffet thee? Come and tell thy God all about it; cast *all* your care upon him, for he careth for you. Think not that God will be angry with thee for asking too much from him, and imagine not that thou wilt insult him by asking him for little things. If thou art a believer in Jesus, God is thy Father, so speak to him as thou wouldst to thine earthly father, only have far more confidence in coming to him than thou wouldst have in approaching the most affectionate earthly parent.

Further, "boldly" also means that *we may come freely*, with simple words. Do not say, "My words are not good enough to present to God; I must get a book of prayers, and try to find suitable words with which to approach the Most High." Oh, do not so! It is true that, in private prayer, in family prayer, and even in public prayer it is better to use a form than not to pray at all. I have often said that it is better to walk with crutches than not to walk at all, but what need have you of crutches; for that is what forms of prayer really are? Your Father in heaven does not want you to come to him in a stiff, formal way, but just to tell out, as simply and naturally as possible, the desires of your heart. If one of my boys wanted a new suit of clothes, or anything else that it was proper for him to have, I should not like him to come with a written request, as if he were presenting a petition to parliament; I should not feel that he loved me very much if he did come in such a fashion as that; but when he asks me for what he wants in a bold, familiar, and yet respectful manner, I am only too pleased to supply his needs.

You who are parents know that you do not make your children offenders for a word. When they first learn to talk to you, they pronounce their words very imperfectly, and make many blunders. They break all the rules of grammar, and their prattle is often so indistinct that strangers who come to your house do not know what they are saying; but you know, mother; you know, father. You understand them all right, and you like to hear them talk like that, it is the natural speech for little children, and there is the accent of love in it that endears it to you. Well, now, go to your God as your little child comes to you. Tell out to him all that is in your heart. Never mind about your words; use such language as your heart dictates, and when you find that you cannot pray as you would, tell him so. Say to him, "O Lord, I cannot put my words together properly; but I pray thee to take my meaning, O my Father; do not judge my prayer by my broken, faulty speech, but read the desires of my heart, and grant them if they are in accordance with thy gracious will!" Perhaps the best prayers of all are those that have no words at all, those that are too deep down in the heart to get shaped into words. We hardly know how they came there, except that we believe God put them there by his Holy Spirit; so he accepts them, even if they are never formed into words.

"Boldly" means, too, that *we may come hopefully*, with full confidence of being heard. It is not a matter of doubt as to whether God hears and answers prayer; if there is any fact in the world that is proved by the testimony of honest men, this is that fact. You know that, at a trial before an earthly judge, there are often many witnesses who give their testimony as to the facts of the case so far as they are known to them, and the weight of their evidence is very largely determined by their personal character. Now, if this was the right time, and I was the counsel in charge of the case, I could bring forward hundreds, and even thousands, of the best men and women who have ever lived,—I mean those who are admitted to be so by all who know them,—honest, straightforward witnesses whose evidence would carry weight in any court of law, who would calmly and deliberately declare that, over and over and over again, God has answered their prayers, so that it has now become with them a matter of course, when they really need anything, to go to God and get it. "Oh!" says someone, "that is only a delusion, there is no such thing as answers to prayer." No, sir, you have no right to say that, for these witnesses have as much right to be believed as you have; possibly, even more, for you may not have the character to support your infidel assertion that these witnesses have to back up their Christian testimony. We can bring forward men who are the equals in learning of any unbeliever, men who are eminent in the ranks of literature, men who are masters of scientific knowledge, yet these very men have been simple as little children in the matter of prayer, and they all testify that God has heard them again and again, and granted their requests. That is a strange "delusion" which is a daily fact in the history of millions, and which has been proved to be true in the lives of millions who are now before the throne of God on high. So let us still pray knowing that God will hear us, and be fully persuaded that he will give us whatever is for his own glory, and our own and others' good. The apostle James reminds us that we must "ask in faith, nothing wavering. For he that wavereth is like a wave of the sea driven with the wind and tossed. For let not that man think that he shall receive any thing of the Lord."

Once more, this word "boldly" means that *we should come perseveringly*, with a fervent importunity that will not be denied. If, at our first coming to the throne of grace, we do not get what we want, let us come again, and keep on coming until we do get it. God sometimes makes us wait for a blessing in order that we may value it all the more when we do receive it. He would have us ask, and seek, and knock again and again, and not be content until we obtain the boon we crave. If we are sure that what we are asking is in accordance with the will of God, let us keep on coming, like the importunate widow came to the unjust judge, until the desire of our heart is granted to us.

I think this is what is meant by coming "boldly unto the throne of grace."

IV. Now, lastly, we have A REASON GIVEN FOR BOLDNESS: "let us *therefore* come boldly unto the throne of grace."

There are a great many other reasons besides the one to which Paul here alludes; I will give them to you in brief.

First, *we are invited to pray.* God would never have invited us to pray if he had not intended to hear and answer us. No right-minded man would invite his fellows to a feast, and then send them away empty. So, the very invitation to us to pray implies that there are blessings waiting for us at the mercy-seat: "let us *therefore* come boldly unto the throne of grace."

Let us remember, too, that grace is for sinners, and *we are invited to come to the throne of grace.* It is only on terms of grace that we can expect to obtain the blessings that we need, but it is to the throne of grace that we are bidden to come. So let the sinner come, for it is the throne of grace. Let the needy saint come, and at the throne of grace "find grace to help in time of need." Let us all come, good or bad, prepared or unprepared, whoever or whatever we may be, let us come boldly because it is the throne of grace, and grace is what we all need.

Let us also remember *the character of the King who sits upon the throne of grace.* He is infinite in mercy and love, and he delights to bless his creatures. He is infinite in power, and is therefore "able to do exceeding abundantly above all that we ask or think." He is infinite in wisdom, and is therefore able to give us whatever is best for us in the best possible way. He is altogether unlimited in his nature, and therefore we cannot exceed his power or his willingness to help us, let our requests be as large as they may. Oh, when I think of what God is as he is revealed in Christ Jesus, and remember that it is he who sits upon the throne of grace, I feel that I may well repeat Paul's exhortation, "Let us *therefore* come boldly unto the throne of grace."

Remember also, O Christian, *your relationship to the King who sits upon the throne of grace*! You are not merely his servant, you are his child; an heir of God, and joint-heir with Jesus Christ. All that you ask for is already yours by right of inheritance, and shall be in your possession in due time. Shall a child tremble in his loving Father's presence? Shall a son act as if he were a slave? Shall I, with tremulous hand, present a petition to my own Father whom I love? If I have perfect love to him, it casts out all fear. So, because we are the children of God by faith in Christ Jesus, "let us *therefore* come boldly unto the throne of grace."

I have already reminded you that *the Holy Spirit has been given to teach us how to pray*. Now the Holy Spirit knows the mind of God, and therefore he never moves us to pray for anything which God does not intend to give us. Prayer is often the shadow of God's coming blessing. Ere the divine decrees are fulfilled, they often cast their blessed shadow across the believer's heart by the power of the Holy Spirit, so that, when the believer prays in the Spirit, he is only asking God to do what he has from all eternity determined to do. If we came to the throne of grace with petitions which we had ourselves prepared, we might well tremble; but when we come with a Spirit-written petition, we may well "come boldly unto the throne of grace."

Then, beloved, there is one sweet thought which should always encourage you to "come boldly unto the throne of grace," and that is, *the many "exceeding great and precious promises" in the Scriptures*. If we had to ask for unpromised boons, we might come tremblingly; but there are promises in God's Word to meet every emergency. "I will never leave thee, nor forsake thee." "As thy days, so shall thy strength be." "Whatsoever ye shall ask the Father in my name, he will give it you." I might go on quoting promises by the hour together, but it will be more profitable for you to search them out for yourselves, especially if you remember what Paul writes concerning the Lord Jesus Christ, "for all the promises of God in him are yea, and in him Amen, unto the glory of God by us." These promises are all the more precious to us because they are free promises, not made to us because of our merits, but solely because of God's grace; and all the promises are made by that faithful God who cannot lie, and by that almighty God who is as able to fulfil the promises as he was to make them; "let us *therefore* come boldly unto the throne of grace."

If we want any more reasons to encourage us to come boldly to the throne, let us remember that *God has already given us his dear Son*, and let us ask again the question that Paul asked so long ago, "He that spared not his own Son, but delivered him up for us all, how shall he not with him also freely give us all things?" You and I, if we are believers in Christ, are already saved with an everlasting salvation; then, after God has given us this greatest of all blessings, will he refuse to bestow upon us the lesser mercies? Brethren and sisters in Christ, as the Lord has already done such great things for us, he cannot turn a deaf ear to our petitions, especially when they are inspired by his own gracious Spirit; "let us *therefore* come boldly unto the throne of grace."

Besides, some of us have had *many years' experience of the power of prayer.* Some of you have had fifty years of soul-enriching commerce with God at the mercy-seat. Do you not remember many times, when you were in deep trouble, and prayer brought you deliverance from it? Do you not recollect some seasons of terrible depression of spirit when prayer brought the sunlight back again to you? Do you not recall that time when you were bereaved, and when, as you stood weeping by the open grave, prayer brought you sweet relief, and dried up your tears? Do you not recollect, when you were in poverty, and prayer obtained bread for you? The ravens did not bring it, nor did a widow woman sustain you, yet you were fed by the God of Elijah in answer to your earnest supplication. What is there that prayer hath not done for us? Oh, the multitude of instances when prayer hath mercy's door unlocked which come to our memory, and they all say, "let us *therefore* come boldly unto the throne of grace."

Now I will close by briefly referring to the reason which the apostle gives why we should come boldly to the throne of grace. I have given you many good reasons, but this is the best reason of all: "We have not a high priest which cannot be touched with the feeling of our infirmities; but was in all points tempted like as we are, yet without sin. Let us *therefore* come boldly unto the throne of grace, that we may obtain mercy, and find grace to help in time of need."

That is to say, we are to come with boldness to the throne because there is pleading for us there a man who is also God, to whom every petition put up by those who trust in him is a very precious thing, which he, as the great representative man before the throne, presents to his Father, for he is God's own dear Son, yea, he is one with the Eternal, and his will is the will of the infinite Jehovah to whom we address our prayers in Christ's name. This glorious God-man Mediator continually presents before his Father his one great sacrifice for sin. There will never be a repetition of it, and it will never need to be offered again, "for by one offering he hath perfected for ever them that are sanctified," that is, those who are set apart unto himself. This one sacrifice he perpetually pleads before the throne, and our prayers therefore ascend to God with the merit of Christ's atoning blood giving them acceptance with his Father. So they must have power with God, for they come before him signed, as it were, with the name of his well-beloved Son. He lays his hand upon each petition, and so leaves the print of the nails upon it, and therefore it must prevail with God.

Remember, too, that this same Jesus Christ was once a man upon earth like ourselves, except that he was "without sin." When your prayer is broken through grief, recollect that he also knew what a broken-hearted prayer meant. The sighs and tears of Gethsemane taught him that. He was made perfect through suffering that he might perfectly sympathize with all his suffering saints. Do not imagine that you can ever get into any condition in which Jesus Christ cannot comprehend you, and consequently cannot sympathize with you. If you are in the depths, as

Jonah was, remember that Jonah was but a type of Christ, who therefore knows all about your present experience, and also knows how to deliver you out of it. If you seem to be altogether deserted by God, and know not why it is so that you have to cry, "My God, my God, why hast thou forsaken me?" that is an experience through which Jesus himself passed. Yea,—

"In every pang that rends the heart
The man of sorrows had a part;"—

so that we have, before the throne of God, a High Priest who is as sympathetic as he is powerful; "let us *therefore* come boldly unto the throne of grace."

Remember, too, that every blessing which you have a right to ask for through Christ is yours already, "for all things are yours; ... things present, or things to come; all are yours; and ye are Christ's; and Christ is God's." Every right prayer that you offer is but putting in a claim for that which is rightly yours through your union to Christ, *therefore* come boldly to the throne of grace because you have such a Pleader to appear there for you, and such a plea to urge with God through him.

Dear brethren and sisters, let us begin to pray more boldly for sinners; let us pray more boldly for London; let us pray more boldly for our country; let us never cease praying to the Lord to send a great revival throughout the whole world. And O ye sinners, ye may come too, for it is "the throne of *grace*" to which we are invited, and it is before that throne that Jesus stands interceding for the transgressors. Come and welcome to Jesus Christ. This is your "time of need." You are full of sin, and need mercy to forgive it, and cleanse you from it. You are full of weakness, and need the help of God. Come to the throne of grace, and ask for his grace to help you in your time of need, and you shall surely have it. God has not left off being a prayer-hearing and prayer-answering God, so come to him; yea, let us all "come boldly unto the throne of grace, that we may obtain mercy, and find grace to help in time of need."

What I have been saying to you I have said far more to myself than to anyone else here; for, if there is one who needs more prayer than all the rest, I am that one, burdened as I am with incessant service and overwhelming responsibilities. Yet, after taking to myself more of the sermon than I pass on to any of you, I venture to say that there is not one person in this building whose condition does not make prayer needful for him. I do not know what the special need of each one of you may be, but I think everyone here, who seriously thinks about the matter, must say, "Well, if there is anybody in this place who can do without prayer, I am not the one; I *must* pray, there is something about my case that drives me to the mercy-seat." Thank God that it is so, but be sure that you go to the throne of grace that you may obtain the help you need. It is a blessed trouble that drives us to the mercy-seat, yet one would scarcely wish to have the kind of trouble that Mr. Fraser, a good old Scotch minister, had. He had a wife who tormented him dreadfully; yet, when someone jestingly said to him that he would not drink her health, he replied, "I hope she will live long, for she has driven me to my knees ten times a day when, otherwise, I might not have prayed." One would not wish to be driven to prayer in such a fashion as that, yet I venture to assert that Mr. Fraser was a gainer by it. Real prayer must make us more like our Master. "Let us *therefore* come boldly unto the throne of grace, that we may obtain mercy, and find grace to help in time of need."

5
ORDER AND ARGUMENT IN PRAYER

"Oh that I knew where I might find him! that I might come even to his seat! I would order my cause before him, and fill my mouth with arguments."—Job 23:3, 4

"Pray for prayer—pray till you can pray; pray to be helped to pray, and give not up praying because thou canst not pray, for it is when thou thinkest thou canst not pray that thou art most praying; and sometimes when thou hast no sort of comfort in thy supplications, it is then that thy heart all broken and cast down is really wrestling and truly prevailing with the Most High."

~

IN Job's uttermost extremity he cried after the Lord. The longing desire of an afflicted child of God is once more to see his Father's face. His first prayer is not, "Oh that I might be healed of the disease which now festers in every part of my body!" nor even, "Oh that I might see my children restored from the jaws of the grave, and my property once more brought from the hand of the spoiler!" but the first and uppermost cry is, "Oh that I knew where I might find HIM—who is my God! that I might come even to his seat!" God's children run home when the storm comes on. It is the heaven-born instinct of a gracious soul to seek shelter from all ills beneath the wings of Jehovah. "He that hath made his refuge God," might serve as the title of a true believer. A hypocrite, when he feels that he has been afflicted by God, resents the infliction, and, like a slave, would run from the master who has scourged him; but not so the true heir of heaven, he kisses the hand which smote him, and seeks shelter from the rod in the bosom of that very God who frowned upon him. You will observe that the desire to commune with God is intensified by the failure of all other sources of consolation. When Job first saw his friends at a distance, he may have entertained a hope that their kindly counsel and compassionate tenderness would blunt the edge of his grief; but they had not long spoken before he cried out in bitterness, "Miserable comforters are ye all." They put salt into his wounds, they heaped fuel upon the flame of his sorrow, they added the gall of their upbraidings to the wormwood of his griefs. In the sunshine of his smile they once had longed to sun themselves, and now they dare to cast shadows upon his reputation, most ungenerous and undeserved. Alas for a man when his wine-cup mocks him with vinegar, and his pillow pricks him with thorns! The patriarch turned away from his sorry friends and looked up to the celestial throne, just as a traveller turns from his empty skin bottle and betakes himself with all speed to the well. He bids farewell to earthborn hopes, and cries, "Oh that I knew where I might find my God!" My brethren, nothing teaches us so much the preciousness of the Creator as when we learn the emptiness of all besides. When you have been pierced through and through with the sentence, "Cursed is he

that trusteth in man, and maketh flesh his arm," then
will you suck unutterable sweetness from the divine
assurance, "Blessed is he that trusteth in the Lord,
and whose hope the Lord is." Turning away with
bitter scorn from earth's hives, where you found no
honey, but many sharp stings, you will rejoice in him
whose faithful word is sweeter than honey or the
honeycomb.

It is further observable that though a good man
hastens to God in his trouble, and runs with all the
more speed because of the unkindness of his fellow
men, yet sometimes the gracious soul is left without
the comfortable presence of God. This is the worst of
all griefs; the text is one of Job's deep groans, far
deeper than any which came from him on account of
the loss of his children and his property: "Oh that I
knew where I might find HIM!" The worst of all losses
is to lose the smile of my God. He now had a
foretaste of the bitterness of his Redeemer's cry, "My
God, my God, why hast thou forsaken me?" God's
presence is always with his people in one sense, so far
as secretly sustaining them is concerned, but his
manifest presence they do not always enjoy. Like the
spouse in the song, they seek their beloved by night
upon their bed, they seek him but they find him not;
and though they wake and roam through the city they
may not discover him, and the question may be sadly
asked again and again, "Saw ye him whom my soul
loveth?" You may be beloved of God, and yet have
no consciousness of that love in your soul. You may
be as dear to his heart as Jesus Christ himself, and yet
for a small moment he may forsake you, and in a little
wrath he may hide himself from you. But, dear
friends, at such times the desire of the believing soul

gathers yet greater intensity from the fact of God's light being withheld. Instead of saying with proud lip, "Well, if he leaveth me I must do without him; if I cannot have his comfortable presence I must fight on as best may be," the soul saith, "No, it is my very life; I must have my God. I perish, I sink in deep mire where there is no standing, and nothing but the arm of God can deliver me." The gracious soul addresseth itself with a double zeal to find out God, and sends up its groans, its entreaties, its sobs and sighs to heaven more frequently and fervently. "Oh that I knew where I might find him!" Distance or labour are as nothing; if the soul only knew where to go she would soon overleap the distance. She makes no stipulation about mountains or rivers, but vows that if she knew where, she would come even to his seat. My soul in her hunger would break through stone walls, or scale the battlements of heaven to reach her God, and though there were seven hells between me and him, yet would I face the flame if I might reach him, nothing daunted if I had but the prospect of at last standing in his presence and feeling the delight of his love. That seems to me to be the state of mind in which Job pronounced the words before us.

But we cannot stop upon this point, for the object of this morning's discourse beckons us onward. It appears that Job's end, in desiring the presence of God, was that he might pray to him. He had prayed, but he wanted to pray as in God's presence. He desired to plead as before one whom he knew would hear and help him. He longed to state his own case before the seat of the impartial Judge, before the very face of the all-wise God; he would appeal from the lower courts, where his friends judged unrighteous judgment, to the Court of King's Bench—the High Court of heaven—there, saith he, "I would order my cause before him, and fill my month with arguments."

In this latter verse Job teaches us how he meant to plead and intercede with God. He does, as it were, reveal the secrets of his closet, and unveils the art of prayer. We are here admitted into the guild of suppliants; we are shown the art and mystery of pleading; we have here taught to us the blessed handicraft and science of prayer, and if we can be bound apprentice to Job this morning, for the next hour, and can have a lesson from Job's Master, we may acquire no little skill in interceding with God.

There are two things here set forth as necessary in prayer—*ordering of our cause, and filling our mouth with arguments*. We shall speak of those two things, and then if we have rightly learned the lesson, a blessed result will follow.

I. First, IT IS NEEDFUL THAT OUR SUIT BE ORDERED BEFORE GOD.

There is a vulgar notion that prayer is a very easy thing, a kind of common business that may be done anyhow, without care or effort. Some think that you have only to reach a book down and get through a certain number of very excellent words, and you have prayed and may put the book up again; others suppose that to use a book is superstitious, and that you ought rather to repeat extemporaneous sentences, sentences which come to your mind with a rush, like a herd of swine or a pack of hounds, and that when you have uttered them with some little attention to what you have said, you have prayed. Now neither of these modes of prayer were adopted by ancient saints. They appear to have thought a great deal more seriously of prayer than many do now-a-days. It seems to have been a mighty business with them, a long-practised exercise, in which some of them attained great eminence, and were thereby singularly blest. They reaped great harvests in the field of prayer, and found the mercy seat to be a mine of untold treasures.

The ancient saints were wont, with Job, to order their cause before God; that is to say, as a petitioner coming into Court does not come there without thought to state his case on the spur of the moment, but enters into the audience chamber with his suit well prepared, having moreover learned how he ought to behave himself in the presence of the great One to whom he is appealing. It is well to approach the seat of the King of kings as much as possible with pre-meditation and preparation, knowing what we are about, where we are standing, and what it is which we desire to obtain. In times of peril and distress we may fly to God just as we are, as the dove enters the cleft of the rock, even though her plumes are ruffled; but in ordinary times we should not come with an unprepared spirit, even as a child comes not to his father in the morning till he has washed his face. See yonder priest; he has a sacrifice to offer, but he does not rush into the court of the priests and hack at the bullock with the first pole-axe upon which he can lay his hand, but when he rises he washes his feet at the brazen laver, he puts on his garments, and adorns himself with his priestly vestments; then he comes to the altar with his victim properly divided according to the law, and is careful to do according to the command, even to such a simple matter as the placing of the fat, and the liver, and the kidneys, and he taketh the blood in a bowl and poureth it in an appropriate place at the foot of the altar, not throwing it just as may occur to him, and kindles the fire not with common flame, but with the sacred fire from off the altar. Now this ritual is all superseded, but the truth which it taught remains the same; our spiritual sacrifices should be offered with holy carefulness. God forbid that our prayer should be a mere leaping out of one's bed and kneeling down, and saying anything that comes first to hand; on the contrary, may we wait upon the Lord with holy fear and sacred awe. See how David prayed when God had blessed him—he went in before the Lord. Understand that; he did not stand outside at a distance, but he went in before the Lord and he sat down—for sitting is not a bad posture for prayer, let who will speak against it— and sitting down quietly and calmly before the Lord he then began to pray, but not until first he had thought over the divine goodness, and so attained to the spirit of prayer. Then by the assistance of the Holy Ghost did he open his mouth. Oh that we oftener sought the Lord in this style! Abraham may serve us as a pattern; he rose up early—here was his willingness; he went three days' journey—here was his zeal; he left his servants at the foot of the hill—here was his privacy; he carried the wood and the fire with him—here was his preparation; and lastly, he built the altar and laid the wood in order, and then took the knife—here was the devout carefulness of his worship. David puts it, "In the morning will I direct my prayer unto thee, and will look up;" which I have frequently explained to you to mean that he marshalled his thoughts like men of war, or that he aimed his prayers like arrows. He did not take the arrow and put it on the bowstring and shoot, and shoot, and shoot anywhere; but after he had taken out the chosen shaft, and fitted it to the string, he took deliberate aim. He looked—looked well—at the white of the target; kept his eye fixed on it, directing his prayer, and then drew his bow with all his strength and let the arrow fly; and then, when the shaft had left his hand, what does he say? "I will look up." He looked up to see where the arrow went, to see what effect it had; for he expected an answer to his prayers, and was not as many who scarcely think of their prayers after they have uttered them. David knew that he had an engagement before him which required all his mental powers; he marshalled up his faculties and went about the work in a workmanlike manner, as one who believed in it and meant to succeed. We should plough carefully and pray carefully. The better the work the more attention it deserves. To be anxious in the shop and thoughtless in the closet is little less than blasphemy, for it is an insinuation that anything will do for God, but the world must have our best.

If any ask what order should be observed in prayer, I am not about to give you a scheme such as many have drawn out, in which adoration, confession, petition, intercession, and ascription are arranged in succession. I am not persuaded that any such order is of divine authority. It is to no mere mechanical order I have been referring, for our prayers will be equally acceptable, and possibly equally proper, in any form; for there are specimens of prayers, in all shapes, in the Old and New Testament. The true spiritual order of prayer seems to me to consist in something more than mere arrangement. It is most fitting for us first to feel that we are now doing something that is real;

that we are about to address ourselves to God, whom we cannot see, but who is really present; whom we can neither touch nor hear, nor by our senses can apprehend, but who, nevertheless, is as truly with us as though we were speaking to a friend of flesh and blood like ourselves. Feeling the reality of God's presence, our mind will be led by divine grace into a humble state; we shall feel like Abraham, when he said, "I have taken upon myself to speak unto God, I that am but dust and ashes." Consequently we shall not deliver ourselves of our prayer as boys repeating their lessons, as a mere matter of rote, much less shall we speak as if we were rabbis instructing our pupils, or as I have heard some do, with the coarseness of a highwayman stopping a person on the road and demanding his purse of him; but we shall be humble yet bold petitioners, humbly importuning mercy through the Saviour's blood. We shall not have the reserve of a slave but the loving reverence of a child, yet not an impudent, impertinent child, but a teachable obedient child, honouring his Father, and therefore asking earnestly, but with deferential submission to his Father's will. When I feel that I am in the presence of God, and take my rightful position in that presence, the next thing I shall want to recognize will be that I have no right to what I am seeking, and cannot expect to obtain it except as a gift of grace, and I must recollect that God limits the channel through which he will give me mercy—he will give it to me through his dear Son. Let me put myself then under the patronage of the great Redeemer. Let me feel that now it is no longer I that speak but Christ that speaketh with me, and that while I plead, I plead his wounds, his life, his death, his blood, himself. This is truly getting into order.

The next thing is to consider what I am to ask for? It is most proper in prayer, to aim at great distinctness of supplication. There is much reason to complain of some public prayers, that those who offer them do not really ask God for anything. I must acknowledge I fear to having so prayed myself, and certainly to having heard many prayers of the kind, in which I did not feel that anything was sought for from God—a great deal of very excellent doctrinal and experimental matter uttered, but little real petitioning, and that little in a nebulous kind of state, chaotic and unformed. But it seems to me that prayer should be distinct, the asking for something definitely and distinctly because the mind has realized its distinct need of such a thing, and therefore must plead for it. It is well not to beat round the bush in prayer, but to come directly to the point. I like that prayer of Abraham's, "Oh that Ishmael might live before thee!" There is the name and the person prayed for, and the blessing desired, all put in a few words,—"Ishmael might live before thee." Many persons would have used a roundabout expression of this kind, "Oh that our beloved offspring might be regarded with the favour which thou bearest to those who," etc. Say "*Ishmael*," if you mean "Ishmael;" put it in plain words before the Lord. Some people cannot even pray for the minister without using such circular descriptives that you might think it were the parish beadle, or somebody whom it did not do to mention too particularly. Why not be distinct, and say what we mean as well as mean what we say? Ordering our cause would bring us to greater distinctness of mind. It is not necessary, my dear brethren, in the closet to ask for every supposable good thing; it is not necessary to rehearse the catalogue of every want that you may have, have had, can have, or shall have. Ask for what you now need, and, as a rule, keep to present need; ask for your daily bread—what you want now—ask for that. Ask for it plainly, as before God, who does not regard your fine expressions, and to whom your eloquence and oratory will be less than nothing and vanity. Thou art before the Lord; let thy words be few, but let thy heart be fervent.

You have not quite completed the ordering; when you have asked for what you want through Jesus Christ. There should be a looking round the blessing which you desire, to see whether it is assuredly a fitting thing to ask; for some prayers would never be offered if men did but think. A little reflection would show to us that some things which we desire were better let alone. We may, moreover, have a motive at the bottom of our desire which is not Christ-like, a selfish motive, which forgets God's glory and caters only for our own ease and comfort. Now although we may ask for things which are for our profit, yet still we must never let our profit interfere in any way with the glory of God. There must be mingled with acceptable prayer the holy salt of submission to the divine will. I like Luther's saying, "Lord, I *will* have my will of thee at this time." "What!" say you, "Like such an expression as that?" I do, because of the next clause, which was, "I will have my will, *for I know that my will is thy will.*" That is well spoken, Luther; but without the last words it would have been wicked presumption. When we are sure that what we ask for is for God's glory, then, if we have power in prayer, we may say, "I will not let thee go except thou bless me:" we may come to close dealings with God, and like Jacob with the angel we may even put it to the wrestle and seek to give the angel the fall sooner than be sent away without the benediction. But we must be quite clear, before we come to such terms as those, that what we are seeking is really for the Master's honour.

Put these three things together, the deep spirituality which recognises prayer as being real conversation with the invisible God—much distinctness which is the reality of prayer, asking for what we know we want—and withal much fervency, believing the thing to be necessary, and therefore resolving to obtain it if it can be had by prayer, and above all these complete submission, leaving it still with the Master's will;—commingle all these, and you have a clear idea of what it is to order your cause before the Lord.

Still prayer itself is an art which only the Holy Ghost can teach us. He is the giver of all prayer. Pray for prayer—pray till you can pray; pray to be helped to pray, and give not up praying because thou canst not pray, for it is when thou thinkest thou canst not pray that thou art most praying; and sometimes when thou hast no sort of comfort in thy supplications, it is then that thy heart all broken and cast down is really wrestling and truly prevailing with the Most High.

II. The second part of prayer is FILLING THE MOUTH WITH ARGUMENTS—not filling the mouth with words nor good phrases, nor pretty expressions, but filling the mouth with arguments. The ancient saints were wont to argue in prayer. When we come to the gate of mercy forcible arguments are the knocks of the rapper by which the gate is opened.

Why are arguments to be used at all? is the first enquiry; the reply being, Certainly not because God is slow to give, not because we can change the divine purpose, not because God needeth to be informed of any circumstance with regard to ourselves or of anything in connection with the mercy asked: the arguments to be used are for our own benefit not for his. He requires for us to plead with him, and to bring forth our strong reasons, as Isaiah saith, because this will show that we feel the value of the mercy. When a man searches for arguments for a thing it is because he attaches importance to that which he is seeking. Again, our use of arguments teaches us the ground upon which we obtain the blessing. If a man should come with the argument of his own merit, he would never succeed; the successful argument is always founded upon grace, and hence the soul so pleading is made to understand intensely that it is by grace and by grace alone that a sinner obtaineth anything of the Lord. Besides, the use of arguments is intended to stir up our fervency. The man who uses one argument with God will get more force in using the next, and will use the next with still greater power, and the next with more force still. The best prayers I have ever heard in our prayer meetings have been those which have been fullest of argument. Sometimes my soul has been fairly melted down when I have listened to brethren who have come before God feeling the mercy to be really needed, and that they must have it, for they first pleaded with God to give it for this reason, and then for a second, and then for a third, and then for a fourth and a fifth, until they have awakened the fervency of the entire assembly. My brethren, there is no need for prayer at all as far as

God is concerned, but what a need there is for it on our own account! If we were not constrained to pray, I question whether we could even live as Christians. If God's mercies came to us unasked, they would not be half so useful as they now are, when they have to be sought for; for now we get a double blessing, a blessing in the obtaining, and a blessing in the seeking. The very act of prayer is a blessing. To pray is as it were to bathe one's-self in a cool purling stream, and so to escape from the heats of earth's summer sun. To pray is to mount on eagle's wings above the clouds and get into the clear heaven where God dwelleth. To pray is to enter the treasure-house of God and to enrich one's-self out of an inexhaustible storehouse. To pray is to grasp heaven in one's arms, to embrace the Deity within one's soul, and to feel one's body made a temple of the Holy Ghost. Apart from the answer prayer is in itself a benediction. To pray, my brethren, is to cast off your burdens, it is to tear away your rags, it is to shake off your diseases, it is to be filled with spiritual vigour, it is to reach the highest point of Christian health. God give us to be much in the holy art of arguing with God in prayer.

The most interesting part of our subject remains; it is a very rapid summary and catalogue of a few of the arguments which have been used with great success with God. I cannot give you a full list; that would require a treatise such as Master John Owen might produce. It is well in prayer to plead with Jehovah *his attributes*. Abraham did so when he laid hold upon God's justice. Sodom was to be pleaded for, and Abraham begins, "Peradventure there be fifty righteous within the city: wilt thou also destroy and not spare the place for the fifty righteous that are therein? That be far from thee to do after this manner, to slay the righteous with the wicked: and that the righteous should be as the wicked, that be far from thee: Shall not the Judge of all the earth do right?" Here the wrestling begins. It was a powerful argument by which the patriarch grasped the Lord's left hand, and arrested it just when the thunderbolt was about to fall. But there came a reply to it. It was intimated to him that this would not spare the city, and you notice how the good man, when sorely pressed, retreated by inches; and at last, when he could no longer lay hold upon justice, grasped God's right hand of mercy, and that gave him a wondrous hold when he asked that if there were but ten righteous there the city might be spared. So you and I may take hold at any time upon the justice, the mercy, the faithfulness, the wisdom, the long-suffering, the tenderness of God, and we shall find every attribute of the Most High to be, as it were, a great battering-ram, with which we may open the gates of heaven.

Another mighty piece of ordnance in the battle of prayer is *God's promise*. When Jacob was on the other side of the brook Jabbok, and his brother Esau was coming with armed men, he pleaded with God not to suffer Esau to destroy the mother and the children, and as a master reason he pleaded, "And thou saidst, Surely I will do thee good." Oh the force of that plea! He was holding God to his word: "Thou saidst." The attribute is a splendid horn of the altar to lay hold upon; but the promise, which has in it the attribute and something more, is a yet mightier holdfast. "Thou saidst." Remember how David put it. After Nathan had spoken the promise, David said at the close of his prayer, "Do as thou hast said." "Do as thou hast said." That is a legitimate argument with every honest man, and has *he* said, and shall he not do it? "Let God be true, and every man a liar." Shall not *he* be true? Shall *he* not keep his word? Shall not every word that cometh out of his lips stand fast and be fulfilled? Solomon, at the opening of the temple, used this same mighty plea. He pleads with God to remember the word which he had spoken to his father David, and to bless that place. When a man gives a promissory note his honour is engaged. He signs his hand, and he must discharge it when the due time comes, or else he loses credit. It shall never be said that God dishonours his bills. The credit of the Most High never was impeached, and never shall be. He is punctual to the moment; he never is before his time, but he never is behind it. You shall search this Book through, and you shall compare it with the experience of God's people, and the two tally from the first to the last; and many a hoary patriarch has said with Joshua in his old age, "Not one good thing hath failed of all that the Lord God hath promised: all hath come to pass." My brother, if you have a divine promise, you need not plead that with an "if" in it; you may plead with a certainty. If for the mercy which you are now asking, you have God's solemnly pledged word, there will scarce be any room for the caution about submission to his will. You know his will: that will is in the promise; plead it. Do not give him rest until he fulfil it. He meant to fulfil it, or else he would not have given it. God does not give his words merely to quiet our noise, and to keep us hopeful for awhile, with the intention of putting us off at last; but when he speaks, he speaks because he means to act.

A third argument to be used is that employed by Moses, *the great name of God*. How mightily did he argue with God on one occasion upon this ground! "What wilt thou do for thy great name? The Egyptians will say, Because the Lord could not bring them into the laud, therefore he slew them in the wilderness." There are some occasions when the name of God is very closely tied up with the history of his people. Sometimes in reliance upon a divine promise, a believer will be led to take a certain course of action. Now, if the Lord should not be as good as his promise, not only is the believer deceived, but the wicked world looking on would say, Aha! aha! Where is your God? Take the case of our respected brother, Mr. Müller, of Bristol. These many years he has declared that God hears prayer, and firm in that conviction, he has gone on to build house after house for the maintenance of orphans. Now, I can very well conceive that, if he were driven to a point of want of means for the maintenance of those thousand or two thousand children, he might very well use the plea, "What wilt thou do for thy great name?" And you, in some severe trouble, when you have fairly received the promise, may say, "Lord, thou hast said, 'In six troubles I will be with thee, and in seven I will not forsake thee.' I have told my friends and neighbours that I put my trust in thee, and if thou do not deliver me now, where is thy name? Arise, O God, and do this thing, lest thy honour be cast into the dust." Coupled with this, we may employ the further argument of *the hard things said by the revilers*. It was well done of Hezekiah, when he took Rabshakeh's letter and spread it before the Lord. Will that help him? It is full of blasphemy, will that help him? "Where are the gods of Arphad and Sepharvaim? where are the gods of the cities which I have overthrown? Let not Hezekiah deceive you, saying that Jehovah will deliver you." Does that have any effect? Oh! yes, it was a blessed thing that Rabshakeh wrote that etter, for it provoked the Lord to help his people. Sometimes the child of God can rejoice when he sees his enemies get thoroughly out of temper and take to reviling. "Now," he says, "they have reviled the Lord himself; not me alone have they assailed, but the Most High himself. Now it is no longer the poor insignificant Hezekiah with his little band of soldiers, but it is Jehovah, the King of angels, who has come to fight against Rabshakeh. Now what wilt thou do, O boastful soldier of proud Sennacherib? Shalt not thou be utterly destroyed, since Jehovah himself has come into the fray? All the progress that is made by Popery, all the wrong things said by speculative atheists and so on, would be by Christians used as an argument with God, why he should help the gospel. Lord; see how they reproach the gospel of Jesus! Pluck thy right hand out of thy bosom! O God, they defy thee! Antichrist thrusts itself into the place where thy Son once was honoured, and from the very pulpits where the gospel was once preached Popery is now declared. Arise, O God, wake up thy zeal, let thy sacred passions burn! Thine ancient foe again prevails. Behold the harlot of Babylon once more upon her scarlet-coloured beast rides forth in triumph! Come, Jehovah, come, Jehovah, and once again show what thy bare arm can do! This is a legitimate mode of pleading with God, for his great name's sake.

So also may we plead *the sorrows of his people.* This is frequently done. Jeremiah is the great master of this art. He says, "Her Nazarites were purer than snow, they were whiter than milk, they were more ruddy in body than rubies, their polishing was of sapphire: their visage is blacker than a coal." "The precious sons of Zion, comparable to fine gold, how are they esteemed as earthen pitchers, the work of the hands of the potter!" He talks of all their griefs and straitnesses in the siege. He calls upon the Lord to look upon his suffering Zion; and ere long his plaintive cries are heard. Nothing so eloquent with the father as his child's cry; yes, there is one thing more mighty still, and that is a moan,—when the child is so sick that it is past crying, and lies moaning with that kind of moan which indicates extreme suffering and intense weakness. Who can resist that moan? Ah! and when God's Israel shall be brought very low so that they can scarcely cry but only their moans are heard, then comes the Lord's time of deliverance, and he is sure to show that he loveth his people. Dear friends, whenever you also are brought into the same condition you may plead your moanings, and when you see a church brought very low you may use her griefs as an argument why God should return and save the remnant of his people.

Brethren, it is good to plead with God *the past*. Ah, you experienced people of God, you know how to do this. Here is David's specimen of it: "Thou *hast* been my help. Leave me not, neither forsake me." He pleads God's mercy to him from his youth up. He speaks of being cast upon his God from his very birth, and then he pleads, "Now also, when I am old and greyheaded, O God, forsake me not." Moses also, speaking with God, says, "Thou *didst* bring this people up out of Egypt." As if he would say, "Do not leave thy work unfinished; thou hast begun to build, complete it. Thou hast fought the first battle; Lord, end the campaign! Go on till thou gettest a complete victory." How often have we cried in our trouble, "Lord, thou didst deliver me in such and such a sharp trial, when it seemed as if no help were near; thou hast never forsaken me yet. I have set up my Ebenezer in thy name. If thou hadst intended to leave me why hast thou showed me such things? Hast thou brought thy servant to this place to put him to shame?" Brethren, we have to deal with an unchanging God, who will do in the future what he has done in the past, because he never turns from his purpose, and cannot be thwarted in his design; the past thus becomes a very mighty means of winning blessings from him.

We may even use our own unworthiness as an argument with God. "Out of the eater comes forth meat, and out of the strong comes forth sweetness." David in one place pleads thus: "Lord, have mercy upon mine iniquity, for it is great." That is a very singular mode of reasoning; but being interpreted it means, "Lord, why shouldest thou go about doing little things? Thou art a great God, and here is a great sinner. Here is a fitness in me for the display of thy grace. The greatness of my sin makes me a platform for the greatness of thy mercy. Let the greatness of thy love be seen in me." Moses seems to have the same on his mind when he asks God to show his great power in sparing his sinful people. The power with which God restrains himself is great indeed. O brothers and sisters, there is such a thing as creeping down at the foot of the throne, crouching low and crying, "O God, break me not—I am a braised reed.

Oh! tread not on my little life, it is now but as the smoking flax. Wilt thou hunt me? Wilt thou come out, as David said, "after a dead dog, after a flea?" Wilt thou pursue me as a leaf that is blown in the tempest? Wilt thou watch me, as Job saith, as though I were a vast sea, or a great whale? Nay, but because I am so little, and because the greatness of thy mercy can be, shown in one so insignificant and yet so vile, therefore, O God, have mercy upon me."

There was once an occasion when the very Godhead of Jehovah made a triumphant plea for the prophet Elijah. On that august occasion, when he had bidden his adversaries see whether their god could answer them by fire, you can little guess the excitement there must have been that day in the prophet's mind. With what stern sarcasm did he say, "Cry aloud: for he is a god; either he is talking, or he is pursuing, or he is in a journey, or peradventure he sleepeth, and must be awakened." And as they cut themselves with knives, and leaped upon the altar, oh the scorn with which that man of God must have looked down upon their impotent exertions, and their earnest but useless cries! But think of how his heart must have palpitated, if it had not been for the strength of his faith, when he repaired the altar of God that was broken down, and laid the wood in order, and killed the bullock. Hear him cry, "Pour water on it. You shall not suspect me of concealing fire; pour water on the victim." When they had done so, he bids them "Do it a second time;" and they did it a second time; and then he says, "Do it a third time." And when it was all covered with water, soaked and saturated through, then he stands up and cries to God, "O God, let it be known that thou only art

God." Here everything was put to the test. Jehovah's own existence was now put, as it were, at stake, before the eyes of men by this bold prophet. But how well the prophet was heard! Down came the fire and devoured not only the sacrifice, but even the wood, and the stones, and even the very water that was in the trenches, for Jehovah God had answered his servant's prayer. We sometimes may do the same, and say unto him, "Oh, by thy Deity, by thine existence, if indeed thou be God, now show thyself for the help of thy people!"

Lastly, the grand Christian argument is *the sufferings, the death, the merit, the intercession of Christ Jesus.* Brethren, I am afraid we do not understand what it is that we have at our command when we are allowed to plead with God for Christ's sake. I met with this thought the other day, it was somewhat new to me, but I believe it ought not to have been. When we ask God to hear us, pleading Christ's name, we usually mean, "O Lord, thy dear Son deserves this of thee; do this unto me because of what he merits." But if we knew it we might go farther. Supposing you should say to me, you who keep a warehouse in the city, "Sir, call at my office, and use my name, and say that they are to give you such a thing." I should go in and use your name, and I should obtain my request as a matter of right and a matter of necessity. This is virtually what Jesus Christ says to us. "If you need anything of God, all that the Father has belongs to me; go and use my name." Suppose you should give a man your cheque-book signed with your own name and left blank, to be filled up as he chose; that would be very nearly what Jesus has done in these words, "If ye ask anything in my name I will give it you." If I had a good name at the bottom of the cheque I should be sure that I should get it cashed when I went to the banker with it; so when you have got Christ's name, to whom the very justice of God hath become a debtor, and whose merits have claims with the Most High, when you have Christ's name there is no need to speak with fear and trembling and bated breath. Oh waver not and let not faith stagger! When thou pleadest the name of Christ thou pleadest that which shakes the gates of hell, and which the hosts of heaven obey, and God himself feels the sacred power of that divine plea.

Brethren, you would do better if you sometimes thought more in your prayers of Christ's griefs and groans. Bring before the Lord his wounds, tell the Lord of his cries, make the groans of Jesus cry again from Gethsemane, and his blood speak again from that frozen Calvary. Speak out and tell the Lord that with such griefs, and cries, and groans to plead, thou canst not take a denial: such arguments as these will speed you.

III. If the Holy Ghost shall teach us how to order our cause, and how to fill our mouth with arguments, the result shall be that WE SHALL HAVE OUR MOUTH FILLED WITH PRAISES. The man who has his mouth full of arguments in prayer shall soon have his mouth full of benedictions in answer to prayer. Dear friend, thou hast thy mouth full this morning, hast thou? what of? Full of complaining? Pray the Lord to rinse thy mouth out of that black stuff, for it will little avail thee, and it will be bitter in thy bowels one of these days. Oh have thy mouth full of prayer, full of it, full of arguments so that there is room for nothing else. Then come with this blessed mouthful, and you shall soon go away with whatsoever you have asked of God. Only delight thou thyself in him, and he will give thee the desire of thy heart.

It is said—I know not how truly—that the explanation of the text, "Open thy mouth wide and I will fill it," may be found in a very singular Oriental custom. It is said that not many years ago—I remember the circumstance being reported—the King of Persia ordered the chief of his nobility, who had done something or other which greatly gratified him, to open his mouth, and when he had done so he began to put into his mouth pearls, diamonds, rubies, and emeralds, till he had filled it as full as it could hold, and then he bade him go his way. This is said to have been occasionally done in Oriental Courts towards great favourites. Now certainly whether that be an explanation of the text or not it is an illustration of it. God says, "Open thy mouth with arguments," and then he will fill it with mercies priceless, gems unspeakably valuable. Would not a man open his mouth wide when he had to have it filled in such a style? Surely the most simple-minded among you would be wise enough for that. Oh! let us then open wide our mouth when we have to plead with God. Our needs are great, let our askings be great, and the supply shall be great too. You are not straitened in him; you are straitened in your own bowels. The Lord give you large-mouthedness in prayer, great potency, not in the use of language, but in employing arguments.

What I have been speaking to the Christian is applicable in great measure to the unconverted. God give thee to see its force, and to fly in humble prayer to the Lord Jesus and to find eternal life in him.

6
THE HOLY SPIRIT'S INTERCESSION

"Likewise the Spirit also helpeth our infirmities: for we know not what we should pray for as we ought: but the Spirit itself maketh intercession for us with groanings which cannot be uttered. And he that searcheth the hearts knoweth what is the mind of the Spirit, because he maketh intercession for the saints according to the will of God."—Romans 8:26, 27

"A mother can translate baby-talk: she comprehends incomprehensible noises. Even so doth our Father in heaven know all about our poor baby talk, for our prayer is not much better."

~

THE Apostle Paul was writing to a tried and afflicted people, and one of his objects was to remind them of the rivers of comfort which were flowing near at hand. He first of all stirred up their pure minds by way of remembrance as to their sonship,—for saith he "as many as are led by the Spirit of God, they are the sons of God." They were, therefore, encouraged to take part and lot with Christ, the elder brother, with whom they had become joint heirs; and they were exhorted to suffer with him, that they might afterwards be glorified with him. All that they endured came from a Father's hand, and this should comfort them. A thousand sources of joy are opened in that one blessing of adoption. Blessed be the God and Father of our Lord Jesus Christ, by whom we have been begotten into the family of grace.

When Paul had alluded to that consoling subject he turned to the next ground of comfort—namely, that we are to be sustained under present trial by hope. There is an amazing glory in reserve for us, and though as yet we cannot enter upon it, but in harmony with the whole creation must continue to groan and travail, yet the hope itself should minister strength to us, and enable us patiently to bear "these light afflictions, which are but for a moment." This also is a truth full of sacred refreshment: hope sees a crown in reserve, mansions in readiness, and Jesus himself preparing a place for us, and by the rapturous sight she sustains the soul under the sorrows of the hour. Hope is the grand anchor by whose means we ride out the present storm.

The apostle then turns to a third source of comfort, namely, the abiding of the Holy Spirit in and with the Lord's people. He uses the word "likewise" to intimate that in the same manner as hope sustains the soul, so does the Holy Spirit strengthen us under trial. Hope operates spiritually upon our spiritual faculties, and so does the Holy Spirit, in some mysterious way, divinely operate upon the new-born faculties of the believer, so that he is sustained under his infirmities. In his light shall we see light: I pray, therefore, that we may be helped of the Spirit while we consider his mysterious operations, that we may not fall into error or miss precious truth through blindness of heart.

The text speaks of "our infirmities," or as many

CHARLES SPURGEON

translators put it in the singular—of "our infirmity." By this is intended our affliction, and the weakness which trouble discovers in us. The Holy Spirit helps us to bear the infirmity of our body and of our mind; he helps us to bear our cross, whether it be physical pain, or mental depression, or spiritual conflict, or slander, or poverty, or persecution. He helps our infirmity; and with a helper so divinely strong we need not fear for the result. God's grace will be sufficient for us; his strength will be made perfect in weakness.

I think, dear friends, you will all admit that if a man can pray, his trouble is at once lightened. When we feel that we have power with God and can obtain anything we ask for at his hands, then our difficulties cease to oppress us. We take our burden to our heavenly Father and tell it out in the accents of childlike confidence, and we come away quite content to bear whatever his holy will may lay upon us. Prayer is a great outlet for grief; it draws up the sluices, and abates the swelling flood, which else might be too strong for us. We bathe our wound in the lotion of prayer, and the pain is lulled, the fever is removed. But the worst of it is that in certain conditions of heart we cannot pray. We may be brought into such perturbation of mind, and perplexity of heart, that we do not know how to pray. We see the mercy-seat, and we perceive that God will hear us: we have no doubt about that, for we know that we are his own favoured children, and yet we hardly know what to desire. We fall into such heaviness of spirit, and entanglement of thought, that the one remedy of prayer, which we have always found to be unfailing, appears to be taken from us. Here, then, in the nick of time, as a very present help in time of trouble, comes in the Holy

Spirit. He draws near to teach us how to pray, and in this way he helps our infirmity, relieves our suffering, and enables us to bear the heavy burden without fainting under the load.

At this time our subjects for consideration shall be, firstly, *the help which the Holy Spirit gives*: secondly, *the prayers which he inspires*; and thirdly, *the success which such prayers are certain to obtain*.

I. First, then, let us consider THE HELP WHICH THE HOLY GHOST GIVES.

The help which the Holy Ghost renders to us meets the weakness which we deplore. As I have already said, if in time of trouble a man can pray, his burden loses its weight. If the believer can take anything and everything to God, then he learns to glory in infirmity, and to rejoice in tribulation; but sometimes we are in such confusion of mind that we know not what we should pray for as we ought. In a measure, through our ignorance, we never know what we should pray for until we are taught of the Spirit of God, but there are times when this beclouding of the soul is dense indeed, and we do not even know what would help us out of our trouble if we could obtain it. We see the disease, but the name of the medicine is not known to us. We look over the many things which we might ask for of the Lord, and we feel that each of them would be helpful, but that none of them would precisely meet our case. For spiritual blessings which we know to be according to the divine will we could ask with confidence, but perhaps these would not meet our peculiar circumstances. There are other things for which we are allowed to ask, but we scarcely know whether, if we had them, they would really serve our turn, and we also feel a diffidence as to praying for them. In praying for temporal things we plead with measured voices, ever referring our petition for revision to the will of the Lord. Moses prayed that he might enter Canaan, but God denied him; and the man that was healed asked our Lord that he might be with him, but he received for answer, "Go home to thy friends." We pray evermore on such matters with this reserve, "Nevertheless, not as I will, but as thou wilt." At times this very spirit of resignation appears to increase our mental difficulty, for we do not wish to ask for anything that would be contrary to the mind of God, and yet we must ask for something. We are reduced to such straits that we must pray, but what shall be the particular subject of prayer we cannot for a while make out. Even when ignorance and perplexity are removed, we know not what we should pray for "as we ought." When we know the matter of prayer, we yet fail to pray in a right manner. We ask, but we are afraid that we shall not have, because we do not exercise the thought, or the faith, which we judge to be essential to prayer. We cannot at times command even the earnestness which is the life of supplication: a torpor steals over us, our heart is chilled, our hand is numbed, and we cannot wrestle with the angel. We know what to pray for as to objects, but we do not know what to pray for *"as we ought."* It is the manner of the prayer which perplexes us, even when the matter is decided upon. How can I pray? My mind wanders: I chatter like a crane; I roar like a beast in pain; I moan in the brokenness of my heart, but oh, my God, I know not what it is my inmost spirit needs; or if I know it, I know not how to frame my petition aright before thee. I know not how to open my lips in thy majestic presence: I am so troubled that I cannot speak. My spiritual distress robs me of the power to pour out my heart before my God. Now, beloved, it is in such a plight as this that the Holy Ghost aids us with his divine help, and hence he is "a very present help in time of trouble."

Coming to our aid in our bewilderment *he instructs us.* This is one of his frequent operations upon the mind of the believer: "he shall teach you all things." He instructs us as to our need, and as to the promises of God which refer to that need. He shows us where our deficiencies are, what our sins are, and what our necessities are; he sheds a light upon our condition, and makes us feel deeply our helplessness, sinfulness, and dire poverty; and then he casts the same light upon the promises of the Word, and lays home to the heart that very text which was intended to meet the occasion—the precise promise which was framed with foresight of our present distress. In that light he makes the promise shine in all its truthfulness, certainty, sweetness, and suitability, so that we, poor trembling sons of men, dare take that word into our mouth which first came out of God's mouth, and then come with it as an argument, and plead it before the throne of the heavenly grace. Our prevalence in prayer lies in the plea, "Lord, do as thou hast said." How greatly we ought to value the Holy Spirit, because when we are in the dark he gives us light, and when our perplexed spirit is so befogged and beclouded that it cannot see its own need, and cannot find out the appropriate promise in the Scriptures, the Spirit of God comes in and teaches us all things, and brings all things to our remembrance, whatsoever our Lord has told us. He guides us in prayer, and thus he helps our infirmity.

But the blessed Spirit does more than this, he will often *direct the mind to the special subject of prayer.* He dwells within us as a counsellor, and points out to us what it is we should seek at the hands of God. We do not know why it is so, but we sometimes find our minds carried as by a strong under current into a particular line of prayer for some one definite object. It is not merely that our judgment leads us in that direction, though usually the Spirit of God acts upon us by enlightening our judgment, but we often feel an unaccountable and irresistible desire rising again and again within our heart, and this so presses upon us, that we not only utter the desire before God at our ordinary times for prayer, but we feel it crying in our hearts all the day long, almost to the supplanting of all other considerations. At such times we should thank God for direction and give our desire a clear road: the Holy Spirit is granting us inward direction as to how we should order our petitions before the throne of grace, and we may now reckon upon good success in our pleadings. Such guidance will the Spirit give to each of you if you will ask him to illuminate you. He will guide you both negatively and positively. Negatively, he will forbid you to pray for such and such a thing, even as Paul essayed to go into Bithynia, but the Spirit suffered him not: and, on the other hand, he will cause you to hear a cry within your soul which shall guide your petitions, even as he made Paul hear the cry from Macedonia, saying, "Come over and help us." The Spirit teaches wisely, as no other teacher can do. Those who obey his promptings shall not walk in darkness. He leads the spiritual eye to take good and steady aim at the very centre of the target, and thus we hit the mark in our pleadings.

Nor is this all, for the Spirit of God is not sent merely to guide and help our devotion, but *he himself "maketh intercession for us"* according to the will of God. By this expression it cannot be meant that the Holy Spirit ever groans or personally prays; but that *he excites intense desire and creates unutterable groanings in us*, and these are ascribed to him. Even as Solomon built the temple because he superintended and ordained all, and yet I know not that he ever fashioned a timber or prepared a stone, so doth the Holy Spirit pray and plead within us by leading us to pray and plead. This he does by arousing our desires. The Holy Spirit has a wonderful power over renewed hearts, as much power as the skilful minstrel hath over the strings among which he lays his accustomed hand. The influences of the Holy Ghost at times pass through the soul like winds through an Eolian harp, creating and inspiring sweet notes of gratitude and tones of desire, to which we should have been strangers if it had not been for his divine visitation. He knows how to create in our spirit hunger and thirst for good things. He can arouse us from our spiritual lethargy, he can warm us out of our luke-warmness, he can enable us when we are on our knees to rise above the ordinary routine of prayer into that victorious importunity against which nothing can stand. He can lay certain desires so pressingly upon our hearts that we can never rest till they are fulfilled. He can make the zeal for God's house to eat us up, and the passion for God's glory to be like a fire within our bones; and this is one part of that process by which in inspiring our prayers he helps our infirmity. True Advocate is he, and Comforter most effectual. Blessed be his name.

The Holy Spirit also divinely operates in *the strengthening of the faith of believers*. That faith is at first of his creating, and afterwards it is of his sustaining and increasing: and oh, brothers and sisters, have you not often felt your faith rise in proportion to your trials? Have you not, like Noah's ark, mounted towards heaven as the flood deepened around you? You have felt as sure about the promise as you felt about the trial. The affliction was, as it were, in your very bones, but the promise was also in your very heart. You could not doubt the affliction, for you smarted under it, but you might almost as soon have doubted that you were afflicted as have doubted the divine help, for your confidence was firm and unmoved. The greatest faith is only what God has a right to expect from us, yet do we never exhibit it except as the Holy Ghost strengthens our confidence, and opens up before us the covenant with all its seals and securities. He it is that leads our soul to cry, "Though my house be not so with God, yet hath he made with me an everlasting covenant ordered in all things and sure." Blessed be the Divine Spirit then, that since faith is essential to prevailing prayer, he helps us in supplication by increasing our faith. Without faith prayer cannot speed, for he that wavereth is like a wave of the sea driven with the wind and tossed, and such an one may not expect anything of the Lord; happy are we when the Holy Spirit removes our wavering, and enables us like Abraham to believe without staggering, knowing full well that he who has promised is able also to perform.

By three figures I will endeavour to describe the work of the Spirit of God in this matter, though they all fall short, and indeed all that I can say must fall infinitely short of the glory of his work. The actual mode of his working upon the mind we may not attempt to explain; it remains a mystery, and it would be an unholy intrusion to attempt to remove the veil. There is no difficulty in our believing that as one human mind operates upon another mind, so does the Holy Spirit influence our spirits. We are forced to use words if we would influence our fellow-men, but the Spirit of God can operate upon the human mind more directly, and communicate with it in silence. Into that matter, however, we will not dive lest we intrude where our knowledge would be drowned by our presumption.

My illustrations do not touch the mystery, but set forth the grace. The Holy Spirit acts to his people somewhat *as a prompter to a reciter*. A man has to deliver a piece which he has learned; but his memory is treacherous, and therefore somewhere out of sight there is a prompter, so that when the speaker is at a loss and might use a wrong word, a whisper is heard, which suggests the right one. When the speaker has almost lost the thread of his discourse he turns his ear, and the prompter gives him the catch-word and aids his memory. If I may be allowed the simile, I would say that this represents in part the work of the Spirit of God in us,—suggesting to us the right desire, and bringing all things to our remembrance whatsoever Christ has told us. In prayer we should often come to a dead stand, but he incites, suggests, and inspires, and so we go onward. In prayer we might grow weary, but the Comforter encourages and refreshes us with cheering thoughts. When, indeed, we are in our bewilderment almost driven to give up prayer, the whisper of his love drops a live coal from off the altar into our soul, and our hearts glow with greater ardour than before. Regard the Holy Spirit as your prompter, and let your ear be opened to his voice.

But he is much more than this. Let me attempt a second simile: he is *as an advocate to one in peril at law*. Suppose that a poor man had a great law-suit, touching his whole estate, and he was forced personally to go into court and plead his own cause, and speak up for his rights. If he were an uneducated man he would be in a poor plight. An adversary in the court might plead against him, and overthrow him, for he could not answer him. This poor man knows very little about the law, and is quite unable to meet his cunning opponent. Suppose one who was perfect in the law should take up his cause warmly, and come and live with him, and use all his knowledge so as to prepare his case for him, draw up his petitions for him, and fill his mouth with arguments,—would not that be a grand relief? This counsellor would suggest the line of pleading, arrange the arguments, and put them into right courtly language. When the poor man was baffled by a question asked in court, he would run home and ask his adviser, and he would tell him exactly how to meet the objector. Suppose, too, that when he had to plead with the judge himself, this advocate at home should teach him how to behave and what to urge, and encourage him to hope that he would prevail,—would not this be a great boon? Who would be the pleader in such a case? The poor client would plead, but still, when he won the suit, he would trace it all to the advocate who lived at home, and gave him counsel: indeed, it would be the advocate pleading for him, even while he pleaded himself. This is an instructive emblem of a great fact. Within this narrow house of my body, this tenement of clay, if I be a true believer, there dwells the Holy Ghost, and when I desire to pray I may ask him what I should pray for as I ought, and he will help me. He will write the prayers which I ought to offer upon the tablets of my heart, and I shall see them there, and so I shall be taught how to plead. It will be the Spirit's own self pleading in me, and by me, and through me, before the throne of grace. What a happy man in his law-suit would such a poor man be, and how happy are you and I that we have the Holy Ghost to be our Counsellor!

Yet one more illustration: it is that of *a father aiding his boy*. Suppose it to be a time of war centuries back. Old English warfare was then conducted by bowmen to a great extent. Here is a youth who is to be initiated in the art of archery, and therefore he carries a bow. It is a strong bow, and therefore very hard to draw; indeed, it requires more strength than the urchin can summon to bend it. See how his father teaches him. "Put your right hand here, my boy, and place your left hand so. Now pull"; and as the youth pulls, his father's hands are on his hands, and the bow is drawn. The lad draws the bow: ay, but it is quite as much his father, too. We cannot draw the bow of prayer alone. Sometimes a bow of steel is not broken by our hands, for we cannot even bend it; and then the Holy Ghost puts his mighty hand over ours, and covers our weakness so that we draw; and lo, what splendid drawing of the bow it is then! The bow bends so easily we wonder how it is; away flies the arrow, and it pierces the very centre of the target, for he who giveth the strength directeth the aim. We rejoice to think that we have won the day, but it was his secret might that made us strong, and to him be the glory of it.

Thus have I tried to set forth the cheering fact that the Spirit helps the people of God.

II. Our second subject is THE PRAYER WHICH THE HOLY SPIRIT INSPIRES, or that part of prayer which is especially and peculiarly the work of the Spirit of God. The text says, "The Spirit itself maketh intercession for us with groanings which cannot be uttered." It is not the Spirit that groans, but we that groan; but as I have shown you, the Spirit excites the emotion which causes us to groan.

It is clear then the prayers which are indited in us by the Spirit of God are *those which arise from our inmost soul.* A man's *heart* is moved when he groans. A groan is a matter about which there is no hypocrisy. A groan cometh not from the lips, but from the heart. A groan then is a part of prayer which we owe to the Holy Ghost, and the same is true of all the prayer which wells up from the deep fountains of our inner life. The prophet cried, "My bowels, my bowels, I am pained at my very heart: my heart maketh a noise in me." This deep ground-swell of desire, this tidal motion of the life-floods is caused by the Holy Spirit. His work is never superficial, but always deep and inward.

Such prayers will rise within us when the mind is far too troubled to let us speak. We know not what we should pray for as we ought, and then it is that we groan, or utter some other inarticulate sound. Hezekiah said, "like a crane or a swallow did I chatter." The psalmist said, "I am so troubled that I cannot speak." In another place he said, "I am feeble and sore broken: I have roared by reason of the disquietness of my heart"; but he added, "Lord, all my desire is before thee; and my groaning is not hid from thee." The sighing of the prisoner surely cometh up into the ears of the Lord. There is real prayer in these "groanings that cannot be uttered." It is the power of the Holy Ghost in us which creates all real prayer, even that which takes the form of a groan because the mind is incapable, by reason of its bewilderment and grief, of clothing its emotion in words. I pray you never think lightly of the supplications of your anguish. Rather judge that such prayers are like Jabez, of whom it is written, that "he was more honourable than his brethren, because his mother bare him with sorrow." That which is thrown up from the depth of the soul, when it is stirred with a terrible tempest, is more precious than pearl or coral, for it is the intercession of the Holy Spirit.

These prayers are sometimes "groanings that cannot be uttered," because *they concern such great things that they cannot be spoken.* I want, my Lord! I want, I want; I cannot tell thee what I want; but I seem to want all things. If it were some little thing, my narrow capacity could comprehend and describe it, but I need all covenant blessings. Thou knowest what I have need of before I ask thee, and though I cannot go into each item of my need, I know it to be very great, and such as I myself can never estimate. I groan, for I can do no more. Prayers which are the offspring of great desires, sublime aspirations, and elevated designs are surely the work of the Holy Spirit, and their power within a man is frequently so great that he cannot find expression for them. Words fail, and even the sighs which try to embody them cannot be uttered.

But it may be, beloved, that *we groan because we are conscious of the littleness of our desire, and the narrowness of our faith*. The trial, too, may seem too mean to pray about. I have known what it is to feel as if I could not pray about a certain matter, and yet I have been obliged to groan about it. A thorn in the flesh may be as painful a thing as a sword in the bones, and yet we may go and beseech the Lord thrice about it, and getting no answer we may feel that we know not what to pray for as we ought; and yet it makes us groan. Yes, and with that natural groan there may go up an unutterable groaning of the Holy Spirit. Beloved, what a different view of prayer God has from that which men think to be the correct one. You may have seen very beautiful prayers in print, and you may have heard very charming compositions from the pulpit, but I trust you have not fallen in love with them. Judge these things rightly. I pray you never think well of *fine* prayers, for before the thrice holy God it ill becomes a sinful suppliant to play the orator. We heard of a certain clergyman who was said to have given forth "the finest prayer ever offered to a Boston audience." Just so! The Boston audience received the prayer, and there it ended. We want the mind of the Spirit in prayer, and not the mind of the flesh. The tail feathers of pride should be pulled out of our prayers, for they need only the wing feathers of faith; the peacock feathers of poetical expression are out of place before the throne of God. "Dear me, what remarkably beautiful language he used in prayer!" "What an intellectual treat his prayer was!" Yes, yes; but God looks at the heart. To him fine language is as sounding brass or a tinkling cymbal, but a groan has music in it. *We* do not like groans: our ears are much too delicate to tolerate such dreary sounds; but not so the great Father of spirits. A Methodist brother cries, "Amen," and you say, "I cannot bear such Methodistic noise"; no, but if it comes from the man's heart God can bear it. When you get upstairs into your chamber this evening to pray, and find you cannot pray, but have to moan out, "Lord, I am too full of anguish and too perplexed to pray, hear thou the voice of my roaring," though you reach to nothing else you will be really praying. When like David we can say, "I opened my mouth and panted," we are by no means in an ill state of mind. All fine language in prayer, and especially all intoning or performing of prayers, must be abhorrent to God; it is little short of profanity to offer solemn supplication to God after the manner called "intoning." The sighing of a true heart is infinitely more acceptable, for it is the work of the Spirit of God.

We may say of the prayers which the Holy Spirit works in us that they are *prayers of knowledge*. Notice, our difficulty is that we know not what we should pray for; but the Holy Spirit does know, and therefore he helps us by enabling us to pray intelligently, knowing what we are asking for, so far as this knowledge is needful to valid prayer. The text speaks of the "mind of the Spirit." What a mind that must be!—the mind of that Spirit who arranged all the order which now pervades this earth! There was once chaos and confusion, but the Holy Spirit brooded over all, and his mind is the originator of that beautiful arrangement which we so admire in the visible creation. What a mind his must be! The Holy

Spirit's mind is seen in our intercessions when under his sacred influence we order our case before the Lord, and plead with holy wisdom for things convenient and necessary. What wise and admirable desires must those be which the Spirit of Wisdom himself works in us!

Moreover, the Holy Spirit's intercession creates *prayers offered in a proper manner*. I showed you that the difficulty is that we know not what we should pray for "as we ought," and the Spirit meets that difficulty by making intercession for us in a right manner. The Holy Spirit works in us humility, earnestness, intensity, importunity, faith, and resignation, and all else that is acceptable to God in our supplications. We know not how to mingle these sacred spices in the incense of prayer. We, if left to ourselves at our very best, get too much of one ingredient or another, and spoil the sacred compound, but the Holy Spirit's intercessions have in them such a blessed blending of all that is good that they come up as a sweet perfume before the Lord. Spirit-taught prayers are offered as they ought to be. They are his own intercession in some respects, for we read that the Holy Spirit not only helps us to intercede but "maketh intercession." It is twice over declared in our text that he maketh intercession for us; and the meaning of this I tried to show when I described a father as putting his hands upon his child's hands. This is something more than helping us to pray, something more than encouraging us or directing us,—but I venture no further, except to say that he puts such force of his own mind into our poor weak thoughts and desires and hopes, that he himself maketh intercession for us, working in us to will and to pray according to his good pleasure.

I want you to notice, however, that *these intercessions of the Holy Spirit are only in the saints.* "He maketh intercession *for us*," and "He maketh intercession *for the saints.*" Does he do nothing for sinners, then? Yes, he quickens sinners into spiritual life, and he strives with them to overcome their sinfulness and turn them into the right way; but in the saints he works with us and enables us to pray after his mind and according to the will of God. His intercession is not in or for the unregenerate. O, unbelievers you must first be made saints or you cannot feel the Spirit's intercession within you. What need we have to go to Christ for the blessing of the Holy Ghost, which is peculiar to the children of God, and can only be ours by faith in Christ Jesus! "To as many as received him to them gave he power to become the sons of God"; and to the sons of God alone cometh the Spirit of adoption, and all his helping grace. Unless we are the sons of God the Holy Spirit's indwelling shall not be ours: we are shut out from the intercession of the Holy Ghost, ay, and from the intercession of Jesus too, for he hath said, "I pray not for the world, but for them which thou hast given me."

Thus I have tried to show you the kind of prayer which the Spirit inspires.

III. Our third and last point is THE SURE SUCCESS OF ALL SUCH PRAYERS.

All the prayers which the Spirit of God inspires in us must succeed, because, first, *there is a meaning in them which God reads and approves.* When the Spirit of God writes a prayer upon a man's heart, the man himself may be in such a state of mind that he does not altogether know what it is. His interpretation of it is a groan, and that is all. Perhaps he does not even get so far as that in expressing the mind of the Spirit, but he feels groanings which he cannot utter, he cannot find a door of utterance for his inward grief. Yet our heavenly Father, who looks immediately upon the heart, reads what the Spirit of God has indited there, and does not need even our groans to explain the meaning. He reads the heart itself: "he knoweth," says the text, "what is the mind of the Spirit." The Spirit is one with the Father, and the Father knows what the Spirit means. The desires which the Spirit prompts may be too spiritual for such babes in grace as we are actually to describe or to express, and yet they are within us. We feel desires for things that we should never have thought of if he had not made us long for them; aspirations for blessings which as to the understanding of them are still above us, yet the Spirit writes the desire on the renewed mind, and the Father sees it. Now that which God reads in the heart and approves of, for the word to "know" in this case includes approval as well as the mere act of omniscience—what God sees and approves of in the heart must succeed. Did not Jesus say, "Your heavenly Father knoweth that you have need of these things before you ask them"? Did he not tell us this as an encouragement to believe that we shall receive all needful blessings? So it is with those prayers which are all broken up, wet with tears, and discordant with sighs and inarticulate expressions and heavings of the bosom, and sobbings of the heart and anguish and bitterness of spirit, our gracious Lord reads them as a man reads a book, and they are written in a character which he fully understands. To give a simple figure: if I were to come into your house I might find there a little child that cannot yet speak plainly. It cries for something, and it makes very odd and objectionable noises, combined with signs and movements, which are almost meaningless to a stranger, but his mother understands him, and attends to his little pleadings. A mother can translate baby-talk: she comprehends incomprehensible noises. Even so doth our Father in heaven know all about our poor baby talk, for our prayer is not much better. He knows and comprehends the cryings, and moanings, and sighings, and chatterings of his bewildered children. Yea, a tender mother knows her child's needs before the child knows what it wants. Perhaps the little one stutters, stammers, and cannot get its words out, but the mother sees what he would say, and takes the meaning. Even so we know concerning our great Father:—

> "He knows the thoughts we mean to speak,
> Ere from our opening lips they break."

Do you therefore rejoice in this, that because the prayers of the Spirit are known and understood of God, therefore they will be sure to speed.

The next argument for making us sure that they will speed is this—that *they are "the mind of the Spirit."* God the ever blessed is one, and there can be no division between the Father, the Son, and the Holy Ghost. These divine persons always work together, and there is a common desire for the glory of each blessed Person of the Divine Unity, and therefore it cannot be conceived without profanity, that anything could be the mind of the Holy Spirit and not be the mind of the Father and the mind of the Son. The mind of God is one and harmonious; if, therefore, the

Holy Spirit dwell in you, and he move you to any desire, then his mind is in your prayer, and it is not possible that the eternal Father should reject your petitions. That prayer which came from heaven will certainly go back to heaven. If the Holy Ghost prompts it, the Father must and will accept it, for it is not possible that he should put a slight upon the ever blessed and adorable Spirit.

But one more word, and that closes the argument, namely, that *the work of the Spirit in the heart is not only the mind of the Spirit which God knows, but it is also according to the will or mind of God*, for he never maketh intercession in us other than is consistent with the divine will. Now, the divine will or mind may be viewed two ways. First, there is the will declared in the proclamations of holiness by the Ten Commandments. The Spirit of God never prompts us to ask for anything that is unholy or inconsistent with the precepts of the Lord. Then secondly, there is the secret mind of God, the will of his eternal predestination and decree, of which we know nothing; but we do know this, that the Spirit of God never prompts us to ask anything which is contrary to the eternal purpose of God. Reflect for a moment: the Holy Spirit knows all the purposes of God, and when they are about to be fulfilled, he moves the children of God to pray about them, and so their prayers keep touch and tally with the divine decrees. Oh would you not pray confidently if you knew that your prayer corresponded with the sealed book of destiny? We may safely entreat the Lord to do what he has himself ordained to do. A carnal man draws the inference that if God has ordained an event we need not pray about it, but faith obediently draws the inference that the God who secretly ordained to give the blessing has openly commanded that we should pray for it, and therefore faith obediently prays. Coming events cast their shadows before them, and when God is about to bless his people his coming favour casts the shadow of prayer over the church. When he is about to favour an individual he casts the shadow of hopeful expectation over his soul. Our prayers, let men laugh at them as they will, and say there is no power in them, are the indicators of the movement of the wheels of Providence. Believing supplications are forecasts of the future. He who prayeth in faith is like the seer of old, he sees that which is yet to be: his holy expectancy, like a telescope, brings distant objects near to him, and things not seen as yet are visible to him. He is bold to declare that he has the petition which he has asked of God, and he therefore begins to rejoice and to praise God, even before the blessing has actually arrived. So it is: prayer prompted by the Holy Spirit is the footfall of the divine decree.

I conclude by saying, see, my dear hearers, the absolute necessity of the Holy Spirit, for if the saints know not what they should pray for as they ought; if consecrated men and women, with Christ suffering in them, still feel their need of the instruction of the Holy Spirit, how much more do you who are not saints, and have never given yourselves up to God, require divine teaching! Oh, that you would know and feel your dependence upon the Holy Ghost that he may prompt you this day to look to Jesus Christ for salvation. It is through the once crucified but now ascended Redeemer that this gift of the Spirit, this promise of the Father, is shed abroad upon men. May he who comes from Jesus lead you to Jesus.

And, then, O ye people of God, let this last thought abide with you,—what condescension is this that this Divine Person should dwell in you for ever, and that he should be with you to help your prayers. Listen to me for a moment. If I read in the Scriptures that in the most heroic acts of faith God the Holy Ghost helpeth his people, I can understand it; if I read that in the sweetest music of their songs when they worship best, and chant their loftiest strains before the Most High God, the Spirit helpeth them, I can understand it; and even if I hear that in their wrestling prayers and prevalent intercessions God the Holy Spirit helpeth them, I can understand it: but I bow with reverent amazement, my heart sinking into the dust with adoration, when I reflect that God the Holy Ghost helps us when we cannot speak, but only groan. Yea, and when we cannot even utter our groanings, he doth not only help us but he claims as his own particular creation the "groanings that cannot be uttered." This is condescension indeed! In deigning to help us in the grief that cannot even vent itself in groaning, he proves himself to be a true Comforter. O God, my God, thou hast not forsaken me: thou art not far from me, nor from the voice of my roaring. Thou didst for awhile leave thy Firstborn when he was made a curse for us, so that he cried in agony, "Why hast thou forsaken me?" but thou wilt not leave one of the "many brethren" for whom he died: thy Spirit shall be with them, and when they cannot so much as groan he will make intercession for them with groanings that cannot be uttered. God bless you, my beloved brethren, and may you feel the Spirit of the Lord thus working in you and with you.

Amen and amen.

7

THE GOLDEN KEY OF PRAYER

"Call unto me, and I will answer thee, and shew thee great and mighty things, which thou knowest not."—Jeremiah 33:3

"If there be anything I know, anything that I am quite assured of beyond all question, it is that praying breath is never spent in vain."

~

SOME of the most learned works in the world smell of the midnight oil; but the most spiritual, and most comforting books and sayings of men usually have a savour about them of prison-damp. I might quote many instances: John Bunyan's *Pilgrim* may suffice instead of a hundred others; and this good text of ours, all mouldy and chill with the prison in which Jeremiah lay, hath nevertheless a brightness and a beauty about it, which it might never have had if it had not come as a cheering word to the prisoner of the Lord, shut up in the court of the prison-house. God's people have always in their worst condition found out the best of their God. He is good at all times; but he seemeth to be at his best when they are at their worst. "How could you bear your long imprisonment so well?" said one to the Landgrave of Hesse, who had been shut up for his attachment to the principles of the Reformation. He replied "The divine consolations of martyrs were with me." Doubtless there is a consolation more deep, more strong than any other, which God keeps for those who, being his faithful witnesses, have to endure exceeding great tribulation from the enmity of man. There is a glorious aurora for the frigid zone; and stars glisten in northern skies with unusual splendour. Rutherford had a quaint saying, that when he was cast into the cellars of affliction, he remembered that the great King always kept his wine there, and he began to seek at once for the wine-bottles, and to drink of the "wines on the lees well refined." They who dive in the sea of affliction bring up rare pearls. You know, my companions in affliction, that it is so. You whose bones have been ready to come through the skin through long lying upon the weary couch; you who have seen your earthly goods carried away from you, and have been reduced well nigh to penury; you who have gone to the grave yet seven times, till you have feared that your last earthly friend would be borne away by unpitying Death; you have proved that he is a faithful God, and that as your tribulations abound, so your consolations also abound by Christ Jesus. My prayer is, in taking this text this morning, that some other prisoners of the Lord may have its joyous promise spoken home to them; that you who are straitly shut up and cannot come forth by reason of present heaviness of spirit, may hear him say, as with a soft whisper in your ears, and in your hearts, "Call upon me, and I will answer thee, and shew thee great and mighty things which thou knowest not."

The text naturally splits itself up into three distinct particles of truth. Upon these let us speak as we are enabled by God the Holy Spirit. *First*, prayer commanded—"Call unto me;" *secondly*, an answer promised—"And I will answer thee;" *thirdly*, faith encouraged—"And shew thee great and mighty things which thou knowest not."

I. The first head is PRAYER COMMANDED.

We are not merely counselled and recommended to pray, but bidden to pray. This is great condescension. An hospital is built: it is considered sufficient that free admission shall be given to the sick when they seek it; but no order in council is made that a man *must* enter its gates. A soup kitchen is well provided for in the depth of winter. Notice is promulgated that those who are poor may receive food on application; but no one thinks of passing an Act of Parliament, compelling the poor to come and wait at the door to take the charity. It is thought to be enough to proffer it without issuing any sort of mandate that men *shall* accept it. Yet so strange is *the infatuation of man* on the one hand, which makes him need a command to be merciful to his own soul, and so marvellous is the condescension of our gracious God on the other, that he issues a command of love without which not a man of Adam born would partake of the gospel feast, but would rather starve than come. In the matter of prayer it is even so. God's own people need, or else they would not receive it, a command to pray. How is this? Because, dear friends, we are very subject to *fits of worldliness*, if indeed that be not our usual state. We do not forget to eat: we do not forget to take the shop shutters down: we do not forget to be diligent in business: we do not forget to go to our beds to rest: but we often do forget to wrestle with God in prayer, and to spend, as we ought to spend, long periods in consecrated fellowship with our Father and our God. With too many professors the ledger is so bulky that you cannot move it, and the Bible, representing their devotion, is so small that you might almost put it in your waistcoat pocket. Hours for the world! Moments for Christ! The world has the best, and our closet the parings of our time. We give our strength and freshness to the ways of mammon, and our fatigue and languor to the ways of God. Hence it is that we need to be commanded to attend to that very act which it ought to be our greatest happiness, as it is our highest privilege to perform, viz. to meet with our God. "Call upon me," saith he, for he knows that we are apt to forget to call upon God. "What meanest thou, oh, sleeper? arise and call upon thy God," is an exhortation which is needed by us as well as by Jonah in the storm.

He understands what *heavy hearts* we have sometimes, when under a sense of sin. Satan says to us, "Why should you pray? How can you hope to prevail? In vain, thou sayest, I will arise and go to my Father, for thou art not worthy to be one of his hired servants. How canst thou see the king's face after thou hast played the traitor against him? How wilt thou dare to approach unto the altar when thou hast thyself defiled it, and when the sacrifice which thou wouldst bring there is a poor polluted one?" O brethren, it is well for us that we are commanded to pray, or else in times of heaviness we might give it up. If God command me, unfit as I may be, I will creep to the footstool of grace; and since he says, "Pray without ceasing," though my words fail me and my heart itself will wander, yet I will still stammer out the wishes of my hungering soul and say, "O God, at least teach me to pray and help me to prevail with thee." Are we not commanded to pray also because of our *frequent unbelief?* Unbelief whispers, "What profit is there if thou shouldst seek the Lord upon such-and-such a matter?" This is a case quite out of the list of those things wherein God hath interposed, and, therefore (saith the devil), if you were in any other position you might rest upon the mighty arm of God; but here your prayer will not avail you. Either it is too trivial a matter, or it is too connected with temporals, or else it is a matter in which you have sinned too much, or else it is too high, too hard, too complicated a piece of business, you have no right to take that before God! So suggests the foul fiend of hell. Therefore, there stands written as an every-day precept suitable to every case into which a Christian can be cast, "Call unto me—call unto me." Art thou sick? Wouldst thou be healed? Cry unto me, for I am a Great Physician. Does providence trouble thee? Art thou fearful that thou shalt not provide things honest in the sight of man? Call unto me! Do thy children vex thee? Dost thou feel that which is sharper than an adder's tooth—a thankless child? Call unto me. Are thy griefs little yet painful, like small points and pricks of thorns? Call unto me! Is thy burden heavy as though it would make thy back break beneath its load? Call unto me! "Cast thy burden upon the Lord, and he shall sustain thee; he shall never suffer the righteous to be moved." In the valley—on the mountain—on the barren rock—in the briny sea, submerged, anon, beneath the billows, and lifted up by-and-by upon the crest of the waves—in the furnace when the coals are glowing—in the gates of death when the jaws of hell would shut themselves upon thee—cease thou not, for the commandment evermore addresses thee with "Call unto me." Still prayer is mighty and must prevail with God to bring thee thy deliverance. These are some of the reasons why the privilege of supplication is also in Holy Scripture spoken of as a duty: there are many more, but these will suffice this morning.

We must not leave our first part till we have made another remark. We ought to be very glad that God hath given us this command *in his word* that it may be sure and abiding. You may turn to fifty passages where the same precept is uttered. I do not often read in Scripture, "Thou shalt not kill;" "Thou shalt not covet." Twice the law is given, but I often read gospel precepts, for if the law be given twice, the gospel is given seventy times seven. For every precept which I cannot keep, by reason of my being weak through the flesh, I find a thousand precepts, which it is sweet and pleasant for me to keep, by reason of the power of the Holy Spirit which dwelleth in the children of God; and this command to pray is insisted upon again and again. It may be a seasonable exercise for some of you to find out how often in scripture you are told to pray. You will be surprised to find how many times such words as these are given; "Call upon me in the day of trouble, and I will deliver thee"—"Ye people, pour out your heart before him." "Seek ye the Lord while he may be found; call ye upon him while he is near." "Ask, and it shall be given you; seek, and ye shall find; knock, and it shall be opened unto you"—

"Watch and pray, lest ye enter into temptation"—
"Pray without ceasing"—"Come boldly unto the
throne of grace," "Draw nigh to God and he will
draw nigh to you." "Continue in prayer." I need not
multiply where I could not possibly exhaust. I pick
two or three out of this great bag of pearls. Come,
Christian, you ought never to question whether you
have a right to pray: you should never ask, "May I be
permitted to come into his presence?" When you
have so many commands, (and God's commands are
all promises, and all enablings,) you may come boldly
unto the throne of heavenly grace, by the new and
living way through the rent veil.

But there are times when God not only
commands his people to pray in the Bible, but he also
commands them to pray directly *by the motions of his
Holy Spirit.* You who know the inner life comprehend
me at once. You feel on a sudden, possibly in the
midst of business, the pressing thought that you *must*
retire to pray. It may be, you do not at first take
particular notice of the inclination, but it comes again,
and again, and again—"Retire and pray!" I find that in
the matter of prayer, I am myself very much like a
water-wheel which runs well when there is plenty of
water, but which turns with very little force when the
brook is growing shallow; or, like the ship which flies
over the waves, putting Out all her canvas when the
wind is favourable, but which has to tack about most
laboriously when there is but little of the favouring
breeze. Now, it strikes me that whenever our Lord
gives you the special inclination to pray, that you
should double your diligence. You ought always to
pray and not to faint; yet when he gives you the
special longing after prayer, and you feel a peculiar

aptness and enjoyment in it, you have, over and above the command which is constantly binding, another command which should compel you to cheerful obedience. At such times I think we may stand in the position of David, to whom the Lord said, "When thou hearest a sound of a going in the tops of the mulberry trees, then "halt thou bestir thyself." That going in the tops of the mulberry trees may have been the footfalls of angels hastening to the help of David, and then David was to smite the Philistines, and when God's mercies are coming, their footfalls are our desires to pray; and our desires to pray should be at once an indication that the set time to favour Zion is come. Sow plentifully now, for thou canst sow in hope; plough joyously now, for thy harvest is sure. Wrestle now, Jacob, for thou art about to be made a prevailing prince, and thy name shall be called Israel. Now is thy time, spiritual merchantmen; the market is high, trade much; thy profit shall be large. See to it that thou usest right well the golden hour, and reap thy harvest while the sun shines. When we enjoy visitations from on high, we should be peculiarly constant in prayer; and if some' other duty less pressing should have the go-bye for a season, it will not be amiss and we shall be no loser; for when God bids us specially pray by the monitions of his Spirit, then should we bestir ourselves in prayer.

II. Let us now take the second head—AN ANSWER PROMISED.

We ought not to tolerate for a minute the ghastly and grievous thought that God will not answer prayer. *His nature*, as manifested in Christ Jesus, demands it. He has revealed himself in the gospel as a God of love, full of grace and truth; and how can he refuse to help those of his creatures who humbly in his own appointed way seek his face and favour? When the Athenian senate, upon one occasion, found it most convenient to meet together in the open air, as they were sitting in their deliberations, a sparrow, pursued by a hawk, flew in the direction of the senate. Being hard pressed by the bird of prey, it sought shelter in the bosom of one of the senators. He, being a man of rough and vulgar mould, took the bird from his bosom, dashed it on the ground and so killed it. Whereupon the whole senate rose in uproar, and without one single dissenting voice, condemned him to die, as being unworthy of a seat in the senate with them, or to be called an Athenian, if he did not render succour to a creature that confided in him. Can we suppose that the God of heaven, whose nature is love, could tear out of his bosom the poor fluttering dove that flies from the eagle of justice into the bosom of his mercy? Will he give the invitation to us to seek his face, and when we. as he knows, with so much trepidation of fear, yet summon courage enough to fly into his bosom, will he then be unjust and ungracious enough to forget to hear our cry and to answer us? Let us not think so hardly of the God of heaven. Let us recollect next, *his past character* as well as his nature. I mean the character which he has won for himself by his past deeds of grace. Consider, my brethren, that one stupendous display of bounty—if I were to mention a thousand I could not give a better illustration of the character of God than that one deed—"He that spared not his own Son, but freely delivered him up for us all"—and it is not my inference only, but the inspired conclusion of an apostle—"how shall he not with him also freely give us all things?" If the Lord did not refuse to listen to my voice when I was a guilty sinner and an enemy, how can he disregard my cry now, that I am justified and saved! How is it that he heard the voice of my misery when my heart knew it not, and would not seek relief, if after all he will not hear me now that I am his child, his friend? The streaming wounds of Jesus are the sure guarantees for answered prayer. George Herbert represents in that quaint poem of his, "*The Bag*," the Saviour saying—

> "If ye have anything to send or write
> (I have no bag, but here is room)
> Unto my Father's hands and sight,
> (Believe me) it shall safely come.
> That I shall mind what you impart
>
> Look, you may put it very near my heart,
> Or if hereafter any of friends
> Will use me in this kind, the door
> Shall still be open; what he sends
> I will present and somewhat more
> Not to his hurt."

Surely, George Herbert's thought Was that the atonement was in itself a guarantee that prayer must be heard, that the great gash made near the Saviour's heart, which let the light into the very depths of the heart of Deity, was a proof that he who sits in heaven would hear the cry of his people. You misread Calvary, if you think that prayer is useless. But, beloved, we have *the Lord's own promise* for it, and he is a God that cannot lie. "Call upon me in, the day of trouble and I will answer thee." Has he not said, "Whatsoever ye shall ask in prayer, believe that ye shall have it and ye shall have it." We cannot pray, indeed, unless we believe this doctrine; "for he that cometh to God must believe that he is, and that he is the rewarder of them that diligently seek him;" and if we have any question at all about whether our prayer will be heard, we are comparable to him that wavereth; "for he who wavereth is like a wave of the sea, driven with the wind and tossed; let not that man think that he shall receive anything of the Lord."

Furthermore, it is not necessary, still it may strengthen the point, if we add that *our own experience* leads us to believe that God will answer prayer. I must not speak for you; but I may speak for myself. If there be anything I know, anything that I am quite assured of beyond all question, it is that praying breath is never spent in vain. If no other man here can say it, I dare to say it, and I know that I can prove it. My own conversion is the result of prayer, long, affectionate, earnest, importunate. Parents prayed for me; God heard their cries, and here I am to preach the gospel. Since then I have adventured upon some things that were far beyond my capacity as I thought; but I have never failed, because I have cast myself upon the Lord. You know as a church that I have not scrupled to indulge large ideas of what we might do for God; and we have accomplished all that we purposed. I have sought God's aid, and assistance, and help, in all my manifold undertakings, and though I cannot tell here the story of my private life in God's work, yet if it were written it would be a standing proof that there is a God that answers prayer. He has heard *my* prayers, not now and then, nor once nor twice, but so many times, that it has grown into a habit with me to spread my case before God with the absolute certainty that whatsoever I ask of God, he will give to me. It is not now a "Perhaps" or a possibility. I know that my Lord answers me, and I dare not doubt, it were indeed folly if I did. As I am sure that a certain amount of leverage will lift a weight, so I know that a certain amount of prayer will get anything from God. As the rain-cloud brings the shower, so prayer brings the blessing. As spring scatters flowers, so supplication ensures mercies. In all labour there is profit, but most of all in the work of intercession: I am sure of this, for I have reaped it. As I put trust in the queen's money, and have never failed yet to buy what I want when I produce the cash, so put I trust in God's promises, and mean to do so till I find that he shall once tell me that they are base coin, and will not do to trade with in heaven's market. But why should speak? O brothers and sisters, you all know in your own selves that God hears prayer; if you do not, then where is your Christianity? where is your religion? You will need to learn what are the first elements of the truth; for all saints, young or old, set it down as certain that he doth hear prayer.

Still remember that prayer is always to be offered in submission to God's will; that when we say, God heareth prayer, we do not intend by that, that he always gives us literally what we ask for. We do mean, however, this, that he gives us what is best for us; and that if he does not give us the mercy we ask for in silver, he bestows it upon us in gold. If he doth not take away the thorn in the flesh, yet he saith, "My grace is sufficient for thee," and that comes to the same in the end. Lord Boling-broke said to the Countess of Huntingdon, "I cannot understand, your ladyship, how you can make out earnest prayer to be consistent with submission to the divine will." "My lord," she said, "that is a matter of no difficulty. If I were a courtier of some generous king, and he gave me permission to ask any favour I pleased of him, I should be sure to put it thus, 'Will your majesty be graciously pleased to grant me such-and-such a favour; but at the same time though I very much desire it, if it would in any way detract from your majesty's honour, or if in your majesty's judgment it should seem better that I did not have this favour, I shall be quite as content to go without it as to receive it.' So you see I might earnestly offer a petition, and yet I might submissively leave it in the king's hands." So with God. We never offer up prayer without inserting that clause, either in spirit or in words, "Nevertheless, not as I will, but as thou wilt; not my will but thine be done." We can only pray without an "if" when we are quite sure that our will must be God's will, because God's will is fully our will. A much-slandered poet has well said—

> "Man, regard thy prayers as a purpose of love to
>   thy soul,
> Esteem the providence that led to them as an
>   index of God's good will;
> So shalt thou pray aright, and thy words shall
>   meet with acceptance.
> Also, in pleading for others, be thankful for the
>   fulness of thy prayer;
> For if thou art ready to ask, the Lord is more
>   ready to bestow.
> The salt preserveth the sea, and the saints uphold
>   the earth;
> Their prayers are the thousand pillars that prop

the canopy of nature.
Verily, an hour without prayer, from some
    terrestrial mind,
Were a curse in the calendar of time, a spot of
    the blackness of darkness.
Perchance the terrible day, when the world must
    rock into ruins,
Will be one unwhitened by prayer—shall He find
    faith on the earth?
For there is an economy of mercy, as of wisdom,
    and power, and means;
Neither is one blessing granted, unbesought from
    the treasury of good:
And the charitable heart of the Being, to depend
    upon whom is happiness,
Never withholdeth a bounty, so long as his
    subject prayeth;
Yea, ask what thou wilt, to the second throne in
    heaven,
It is thine, for whom it was appointed; there is no
    limit unto prayer:
But and if thou cease to ask, tremble, thou self-
    suspended creature,
For thy strength is cut off as was Samson's: and
    the hour of thy doom is come."

III. I come to our third point, which I think is full
of encouragement to all those who exercise the
hallowed art of prayer: ENCOURAGEMENT TO FAITH,
"I will shew thee great and mighty things which thou
knowest not."

Let us just remark that this was originally spoken
to a prophet in prison; and, therefore, it applies in the
first place to *every teacher;* and, indeed, as every teacher

must be a learner, it has a bearing upon *every learner* in divine truth. The best way by which a prophet and teacher and learner can know the reserved truths, the higher and more mysterious truths of God, is by waiting upon God in prayer. I noticed very specially yesterday in reading the Book of the Prophet Daniel, how Daniel found out Nebuchadnezzar's dream. The soothsayers, the magicians, the astrologers of the Chaldees, brought out their curious books and their strange-looking instruments, and began to mutter their *abracadabra* and all sorts of mysterious incantations, but they all failed. What did Daniel do? He set himself to prayer, and knowing that the prayer of a united body of men has more prevalence than the prayer of one, we find that Daniel called together his brethren, and bade them unite with him in earnest prayer that God would be pleased of his infinite mercy to open up the vision. "Then Daniel went to his house and made the thing known to Hananiah, Mishael, and Azariah, his companions, that they would desire mercies of the God of heaven concerning this secret, that Daniel and his fellows should not perish with the rest of the wise men of Babylon." And in the case of John, who was the Daniel of the New Testament, you remember he saw a book in the right hand of him that sat on the throne—a book sealed with seven seals which none was found worthy to open or to look thereon. What did John do? The book was by-and-by opened by the Lion of the Tribe of Judah, who had prevailed to open the book; but it is written first before the book was opened, "I wept much." Yes, and the tears of John which were his liquid prayers, were, as far as he was concerned, the sacred keys by which the folded book was opened.

Brethren in the ministry, you who are teachers in the Sabbath school, and all of you who are learners in the college of Christ Jesus, I pray you remember that prayer is your best means of study: like Daniel you shall understand the dream, and the interpretation thereof, when you have sought unto God; and like John you shall see the seven seals of precious truth unloosed, after that you have wept much. "Yea, if thou criest after knowledge, and liftest up the voice for understanding; if thou seekest her as silver, and searchest for her as for hid treasures; then shalt thou understand the fear of the Lord and find the knowledge of God." Stones are not broken, except by an earnest use of the hammer; and the stone-breaker usually goes down on his knees. Use the hammer of diligence, and let the knee of prayer be exercised, too, and there is not a stony doctrine in Revelation which is useful for you to understand, which will not fly into shivers under the exercise of prayer and faith. *"Bene orasse est bene studuisse"* was a wise sentence of Luther, which has been so often quoted, that we hardly venture but to hint at it. "To have prayed well is to have studied well." You may force your way through anything with the leverage of prayers. Thoughts and reasonings may be like the steel wedges which may open a way into truth; but prayer is the lever, the prise which forces open the iron chest of sacred mystery, that we may get the treasure that is hidden therein for those who can force their way to reach it. The kingdom of heaven still suffereth violence, and the violent taketh it by force. Take care that ye work away with the mighty implement of prayer, and nothing can stand against you.

We must not, however, stop there. We have applied the text to only one case; it is applicable to a hundred. We single out another. *The saint may expect to discover deeper experience* and to know more of the higher spiritual life, by being much in prayer. There are different translations of my text. One version renders it, "I will shew thee great and fortified things which thou knowest not." Another reads it. "Great and reserved things which thou knowest not." Now, all the developments of spiritual life are not alike easy of attainment. There are the common frames and feelings of repentance, and faith, and joy, and hope, which are enjoyed by the entire family: but there is an upper realm of rapture, of communion, and conscious union with Christ, which is far from being the common dwelling-place of believers. All believers see Christ; but all believers do not put their fingers into the prints of the nails, nor thrust their hand into his side. We have not all the high privilege of John to lean upon Jesus' bosom, nor of Paul, to be caught up into the third heaven. In the ark of salvation we find a lower, second, and third storey; all are in the ark, but all are not in the same storey. Most Christians, as to the river of experience, are only up to the ancles; some others have waded till the stream is up to the knees; a few find it breast-high; and but a few—oh! how few!—find it a river to swim in, the bottom of which they cannot touch. My brethren, there are heights in experimental knowledge of the things of God which the eagle's eye of acumen and philosophic thought hath never seen; and there are secret paths which the lion's whelp of reason and judgment hath not as yet learned to travel. God alone can bear us there; but the chariot in which he takes us up, and the fiery steeds with which that chariot is dragged, are prevailing prayers. Prevailing prayer is victorious over the God of mercy "By his strength he had power with God: yea, he had power over the angel, and prevailed: he wept, and made supplication unto him: he found him in Beth-el, and there he spake with us." Prevailing prayer takes the Christian to Carmel, and enables him to cover heaven with clouds of blessing, and earth with floods of mercy. Prevailing prayer bears the Christian aloft to Pisgah and shows him the inheritance reserved; ay, and it elevates him to Tabor and transfigures him, till in the likeness of his Lord, as he is, so are we also in this world. If you would reach to something higher than ordinary grovelling experience, look to the Rock that is higher than you, and look with the eye of faith through the windows of importunate prayer. To grow in experience then, there must be much prayer.

You must have patience with me while I apply this text to two or three more cases. It is certainly true of *the sufferer under trial:* if he waits upon God in prayer much he shall receive greater deliverances than he has ever dreamed of—"great and mighty things which thou knowest not." Here is Jeremiah's testimony:— "Thou drewest near in the day that I called upon thee: thou saidst, Fear not. O Lord, thou hast pleaded the causes of my soul; thou hast redeemed my life." And David's is the same:—"I called upon the Lord in distress: the Lord answered me, and set me in a large place.... I will praise thee: for thou hast heard me, and art become my salvation." And yet again:— "Then they cried unto the Lord in their trouble, and he delivered them out of their distresses. And he led them forth by the right way, that they might go to a city of habitation." "My husband is dead," said the poor woman, "and my creditor is come to take my two sons as bondsmen." She hoped that Elijah would possibly say, "What are your debts? I will say them." Instead of that, he multiplies her oil till it is written, "Go thou and pay thy debts, and"—what was the "and?"—"live thou and thy children upon the rest." So often it will happen that God will not only help his people through the miry places of the way, so that they may just stand on the other side of the slough, but he will bring them safely far on the journey. That was a remarkable miracle, when in the midst of the storm, Jesus Christ came walking upon the sea, the disciples received him into the ship, and not only was the sea calm, but it is recorded, "Immediately the ship was at the land whither they went." That was a mercy over and above what they asked. I sometimes hear you pray and make use of a quotation which is not in the Bible:—"He is able to do exceeding abundantly above what we *can* ask or even think." It is not so written in the Bible. I do not know what we can ask or what we can think. But it is said, "He is able to do exceeding abundantly above what we ask or even think." Let us then, dear friends, when we are in great trial only say, "Now I am in prison; like Jeremiah I will pray as he did, for I have God's command to do it; and I will look out as he did, expecting that he will show me reserved mercies which I know nothing of at present." He will not merely bring his people through the battle, covering their heads in it, but he will bring them forth with banners waving, to divide the spoil with the mighty, and to claim their portion with the strong. Expect great things of a God who gives such great promises as these.

Again, *here is encouragement for the worker.* Most of you are doing something for Christ; I am happy to be able to say this, knowing that I do not flatter you. My dear friends, wait upon God much in prayer, and you have the promise that he will do greater things for you than you know of. We know not how much capacity for usefulness there may be in us. That ass's jaw-bone lying there upon the earth, what can it do? Nobody knows what it can do. It gets into Samson's hands, what can it *not* do? No one knows what it cannot do now that a Samson wields it. And you, friend, have often thought yourself to be as contemptible as that bone, and you have said, "What can I do?" Ay, but when Christ by his Spirit grips you, what can you not do? Truly you may adopt Paul's language and say, "I can do all things through Christ who strengtheneth me." However, do not depend upon prayer without effort. In a certain school there was one girl who knew the Lord, a very gracious, simple-hearted, trustful child. As usual, grace developed itself in the child according to the child's position. Her lessons were always best said of any in the class. Another girl said to her, "How is it that your lessons are always so well said?" "I pray God to help me," she said, "to learn my lesson." Well thought the other, "Then I will do the same." The next morning when she stood up in the class she knew nothing; and when she was in disgrace she complained to the other, "Why I prayed God to help me learn my lesson and I do not know anything of it. What is the use of prayer?" "But did you sit down and try to learn it?" "Oh, no," she said, "I never looked at the book." "Ah," then said the other, "I asked God to help me to learn my lesson; but I then sat down to it studiously, and I kept at it till I knew it well, and I learned it easily, because my earnest desire, which I had expressed to God was, help me to be diligent in endeavouring to do my duty." So is it with some who come up to prayer-meetings and pray, and then they fold their arms and go away hoping that God's work will go on. Like the negro woman singing "Fly abroad, thou mighty gospel," but not putting a penny in the plate; so that her friend touched her and said, "But how can it fly if you don't give it wings to fly with?" There be many who appear to be very mighty in prayer, wondrous in supplications; but then they require God to do what they can do themselves, and, therefore, God does nothing at all for them. "I shall leave my camel untied," said an Arab once to Mahomet, "and trust to providence." "Tie it up tight," said Mahomet, "and then trust to providence." So you that say, "I shall pray and trust my Church, or my class, or my work to God's goodness," may rather hear the voice of experience and wisdom which says, "Do thy best; work as if all rested upon thy toil; as if thy own arm would bring thy salvation;" "and when thou hast done all, cast thy self on him without whom it is in vain to rise up early and to sit up late, and to eat the bread of carefulness; and if he speed thee give him the praise."

I shall not detain you many minutes longer, but I want to notice that this promise ought to prove useful for the comforting of those who are intercessors for others. You who are calling upon God to save your children, to bless your neighbours, to remember your husbands or your wives in mercy, may take comfort from this, "I will shew thee great and mighty things, which thou knowest not." A celebrated minister in the last century, one Mr. Bailey, was the child of a godly mother. This mother had almost ceased to pray for her husband, who was a man of a most ungodly stamp, and a bitter persecutor. The mother prayed for her boy, and while he was yet eleven or twelve years of age, eternal mercy met with him. So sweetly instructed was the child in the things of the kingdom of God, that the mother requested him—and for some time he always did so—to conduct family prayer in the house. Morning and evening this little one laid open the Bible; and though the father would not deign to stop for the family prayer, yet on one occasion he was rather curious to know "what sort of an out the boy would make of it," so he stopped on the other side of the door, and God blessed the prayer of his own child under thirteen years of age to his conversion. The mother might well have read my text with streaming eyes, and said, "Yes, Lord, thou hast shewn me great and mighty things which I knew not: thou hast not only saved my boy, but through my boy thou hast brought my husband to the truth." You cannot guess how greatly God will bless you. Only go and stand at his door, you cannot tell what is in reserve for you. If you do not beg at all, you will get nothing; but if you beg he may not only give you, as it were, the bones and broken meat, but he may say to the servant at his table, "Take thou that dainty meat, and set that before the poor man." Ruth went to glean; she expected to get a few good ears: but Boaz said, "Let her glean even among the sheaves, and rebuke her not;" he said moreover to her, "At mealtime come thou hither, and eat of the bread, and dip thy morsel in the vinegar." Nay, she found a husband where she only expected to find a handful of barley. So in prayer for others, God may give us such mercies that we shall be astounded at them, since we expected but little. Hear what is said of Job, and learn its lesson, "And the Lord said, My servant Job shall pray for you: for him will I accept: lest I deal with you after your folly, in that ye have not spoken of me the thing which is right, like my servant Job.... And the Lord turned the captivity of Job, when he prayed for his friends: also the Lord gave Job twice as much as he had before."

Now, this word to close with. Some of you are seekers for your own conversion. God has quickened you to solemn prayer about your own souls. You are not content to go to hell, you want heaven; you want washing in the precious blood; you want eternal life. Dear friends, I pray you take this text—God himself speaks it to you—"Call unto me, and I will answer thee, and shew thee great and mighty things, which thou knowest not." At once take God at his word. Get home, go into your chamber and shut the door, and try him. Young man, I say, try the Lord. Young woman, prove him, see whether he be true or not. If God be true, you cannot seek mercy at his hands through Jesus Christ and get a negative reply. He must, for his own promise and character bind him to it, open mercy's gate to you who knock with all your heart. God help you, believing in Christ Jesus, to cry aloud unto God, and his answer of peace is already on the way to meet you. You shall hear him say, "Your sins which are many are all forgiven."

The Lord bless you for his love's sake. Amen.

NOTE.—In a former sermon, while denouncing the error of the "Non-confession of sin by believers," we wrongly imputed that gross heresy to the Plymouth Brethren. We have since learned that the persons to whom we alluded have been expelled from that body, and we therefore desire to exonerate the community from a fault of which they are not guilty. We are sorry to have made this charge, as it is far from our wish to speak evil of any, but we were not aware of the expulsion of the guilty persons.

8
PRAYER PERFUMED WITH PRAISE

"In everything by prayer and supplication with thanksgiving let your requests be made known unto God."—Philippians 4:6

"You shall get your answers to prayer when you multiply your thanksgivings in all your prayers and supplications: rest you sure of that."

~

ACCORDING to the text, we are both by prayer and supplication to make known our requests unto God. If any distinction be intended here, I suppose that by prayer is meant the general act of devotion and the mention of our usual needs; and by supplication I think would be intended our distinct entreaties and special petitions. We are to offer the general prayer common to all the saints, and we are to add thereto the special and definite petitions which are peculiar to ourselves. We are to worship in prayer, for God is to be adored by all his saints, and then we are to beseech his favours for ourselves, according to the words of the text, letting our requests be made known unto God. Do not forget this second form of worship.

There is a good deal of generalizing in prayer, and God forbid that we should say a word against it, so far as it is sincere worship, but we want to have more of specific, definite pleading with God, asking him for such-and-such things, with a clear knowledge of what we ask. You will hear prayers at prayer-meetings, in which everything is asked in general but nothing in particular, and yet the reality and heartiness of prayer will often be best manifested by the putting up of requests for distinct blessings. See how Abraham, when he went to worship the Lord, did not merely adore him, and in general pray for his glory, but on a special occasion he pleaded concerning the promised heir, at another time he cried, "O that Ishmael might live before thee," and on one special occasion he interceded for Sodom. Elijah, when on the top of Carmel, did not pray for all the blessings of providence in general, but for rain, for rain there and then. He knew what he was driving at, kept to his point, and prevailed. So, my beloved friends, we have many wants which are so pressing as to be very distinct and definite, and we ought to have just so many clearly defined petitions which we offer unto God by way of supplication, and for the divine answers to these we are bound to watch with eager expectancy, so that when we receive them we may magnify the Lord.

The point to which I would draw your attention is this: that whether it be the general prayer or the specific supplication we are to offer either or both "with thanksgiving." We are to pray about everything, and with every prayer we must blend our thanksgivings. Hence it follows that we ought always to be in a thankful condition of heart: since we are to pray without ceasing, and are not to pray without thanksgiving, it is clear that we ought to be always ready to give thanks unto the Lord. We must say with the Psalmist, "Thus will I bless thee while I live, I will lift up my hands in thy name." The constant tenor and spirit of our lives should be adoring gratitude, love, reverence, and thanksgiving to the Most High.

This blending of thanks with devotion is always to be maintained. Always must we offer prayer and supplication *with* thanksgiving. No matter though the prayer should struggle upward out of the depths, yet must its wings be silvered o'er with thanksgiving. Though the prayer were offered upon the verge of death, yet in the last few words which the trembling lips can utter there should be notes of gratitude as well as words of petition. The law saith, "With all thy sacrifices thou shalt offer salt," and the gospel says with all thy prayers thou shalt offer praise. "One thing at a time" is said to be a wise proverb, but for once I must venture to contradict it, and say that two things at a time are better, when the two are prayer and thanksgiving. These two holy streams flow from one common source, the Spirit of life which dwells within us; and they are utterances of the same holy fellowship with God; and therefore it is right that they should mingle as they flow, and find expression in the same holy exercise. Supplication and thanksgiving so naturally run into each other that it would be difficult to keep them separate: like kindred colours, they shade off into each other. Our very language seems to indicate this, for there is small difference between the words "to pray," and "to praise." A psalm may be either prayer or praise, or both; and there is yet another form of utterance which is certainly prayer, but is used as praise, and is really both. I refer to that joyous Hebrew word which has been imported into all Christian languages, "Hosanna," Is it a prayer? Yes. "Save, Lord." Is it not praise? Yes; for it is tantamount to "God save the king," and it is used to extol the Son of David. While we are here on earth we should never attempt to make such a distinction between prayer and praise that we should either praise without prayer or pray without praise; but with every prayer and supplication we should mingle thanksgiving, and thus make known our requests unto God.

This commingling of precious things is admirable. It reminds me of that verse in the Canticles where the king is described as coming up from the wilderness in his chariot, "like pillars of smoke, perfumed with myrrh and frankincense, with all powders of the merchant." There is the myrrh of prayer, and the frankincense of praise. So, too, the holy incense of the sanctuary yielded the smoke of prayer which filled the holy place, but with it there was the sweet perfume of choice spices, which may be compared to praise. Prayer and praise are like the two cherubim on the ark, they must never be separated. In the model of prayer which our Saviour has given us, saying, "After this manner pray ye," the opening part of it is rather praise than prayer:—"Our Father which art in heaven, hallowed be thy name," and the closing part of it is praise, where we say, "For thine is the kingdom, the power, and the glory, for ever and ever. Amen." David, who is the great tutor and exemplar of the church as to her worship, being at once her poet and her preacher, takes care in almost every psalm, though the petition may be agonising, to mingle exquisite praise, take, for instance, that psalm of his after his great sin with Bathsheba. There one would think, with sighs and groans and tears so multiplied, he might have almost forgotten or have feared to offer thanksgiving while he was trembling under a sense of wrath; and yet ere the psalm that begins "Have mercy upon me, O God," can come to a conclusion the psalmist has said, "O Lord, open thou my lips, and my mouth shall show forth thy praise," and he cannot pen the last word without beseeching the Lord to build the walls of Jerusalem, adding the promise, "then shalt thou be pleased with the sacrifices of righteousness, with burnt offering and whole burnt offering: then shalt they offer bullocks upon thine altar." I need not stop to quote other instances, but it is almost always the case that David by the fire of prayer warms himself into praise. He begins low, with many a broken note of complaining, but he mounts and glows, and, like the lark, sings as he ascends. When at first his harp is muffled he warbles a few mournful notes and becomes excited, till he cannot restrain his hand from that well-known and accustomed string which he had reserved for the music of praise alone. There is a passage in the eighteenth Psalm, at the third verse, in which indeed he seems to have caught the very idea which I want to fix upon your minds this morning. "I will call upon the Lord, who is worthy to be praised: so shall I be saved from mine enemies." He was in such a condition that he says, "The sorrows of death compassed me, and the floods of ungodly men made me afraid. The sorrows of hell compassed me about: the snares of death prevented me." Driven by distress, he declares that he will call upon the Lord, that is, with utterances of prayer; but he does not alone regard his God as the object of prayer, but as one who is to be praised. "I will call upon the Lord, who is worthy to be praised"; and then, as if inspired to inform us of the fact that the blending of thanksgiving with prayer renders it infallibly effectual, as I shall have to show you it does, he adds, "So shall I be saved from mine enemies."

Now, if this habit of combining thanksgiving with prayer is found in the Old Testament saints, we have a right to expect it yet more in New Testament believers, who in clearer light perceive fresh reasons for thanksgiving; but I shall give you no instance except that of the writer of my text. Does he not tell us in the present chapter that those things which we have seen in him we are to do, for his life was agreeable with his teaching? Now, observe, how frequently he commences his epistles with a blending of supplication and thanksgiving. Turn to the Romans, and note in the first chapter, at the eighth and ninth verses, this fusion of the precious metals— "First, I thank my God through Jesus Christ for you all, that your faith is spoken of throughout the whole world. For God is my witness, whom I serve with my spirit in the gospel of his Son, that without ceasing I make mention of you always in my prayers." There is "I thank my God," and "I make mention of you always in my prayers." This was not written with a special eye to the precept of our text; it was natural to Paul so to thank God when he prayed. Look at the Epistle to the Colossians, in the first chapter, at the third verse, "We give thanks to God and the Father of our Lord Jesus Christ, praying always for you." To the same effect we read in the first Epistle to the

Thessalonians, chapter 1, verse 2—"We give thanks to God always for you all, making mention of you in our prayers." Look also at the second of Timothy, 1:3—"I thank God, whom I serve from my forefathers with pure conscience, that without ceasing I have remembrance of thee in my prayers night and day." And if it be so in other epistles we are not at all surprised to find it so in the Philippian epistle itself, for so we read when we turn to its first chapter, at the third and fourth verses—"I thank my God upon every remembrance of you, always in every prayer of mine for you all making request with joy." Nor need I confine you to the language of Paul's epistle, since it is most noteworthy that in Philippi itself (and those to whom he wrote must have remembered the incident) Paul and Silas prayed and sang praises unto God at midnight, so that the prisoners heard them. It is clear that Paul habitually practised what he here enjoins. His own prayers had not been offered without thanksgiving; what God hath joined together he had never put asunder.

With this as a preface, I invite you to consider, carefully and prayerfully, first, *the grounds of thanksgiving in prayer;* secondly, *the evil of its absence;* and thirdly, *the result of its presence.*

I. First, then, there are REASONS FOR MINGLING THANKSGIVING WITH PRAYER. In the nature of things it ought to be so. We have abundant cause, my brethren, for thanksgiving at all times. We do not come to God in prayer as if he had left us absolutely penniless, and we cried to him like starving prisoners begging through prison bars. We do not ask as if we had never received a single farthing of God before, and hardly thought we should obtain anything now;

but on the contrary, having been already the recipients of immense favours, we come to a God who abounds in lovingkindness, who is willing to bestow good gifts upon us, and waits to be gracious to us. We do not come to the Lord as slaves to an unfeeling tyrant craving for a boon, but as children who draw nigh to a loving father, expecting to receive abundantly from his liberal hands. Thanksgiving is the right spirit in which to come before the God who daily loadeth us with benefits. Bethink you for awhile what cause you have for thanksgiving in prayer.

And first you have this, that such a thing as prayer is possible, that a finite creature can speak with the infinite Creator, that a sinful being can have audience with the thrice holy Jehovah. It is worthy of thanksgiving that God should have commanded prayer and encouraged us to draw near unto him; and that moreover he should have supplied all things necessary to the sacred exercise. He has set up a mercy seat, blood besprinkled; and he has prepared a High Priest, ever living to make intercession; and to these he has added the Holy Ghost to help our infirmities and to teach us what we should pray for as we ought. Everything is ready, and God waits for us to enquire at his hands. He has not only set before us an open door and invited us to enter, but he has given us the right spirit with which to approach. The grace of supplication is poured out upon us and wrought in us by the Holy Ghost. What a blessing it is that we do not attempt prayer with a peradventure, as if we were making a doubtful experiment, nor do we come before God as a forlorn hope, desperately afraid that he will not listen to our cry; but he has ordained prayer to be the ordinary commerce of heaven and earth, and sanctioned it in the most solemn manner. Prayer may climb to heaven, for God has himself prepared the ladder and set it down just by the head of his lonely Jacob, so that though that head be pillowed on a stone it may rest in peace. Lo, at the top of that ladder is the Lord himself in his covenant capacity, receiving our petitions and sending his attendant angels with answers to our requests. Shall we not bless God for this?

Let us praise his name, dear friends, also especially that you and I are still spared to pray and permitted to pray. What if we are greatly afflicted, yet it is of the Lord's mercy that we are not consumed. If we had received our deserts we should not now have been on praying ground and pleading terms with him. But let it be for our comfort and to God's praise that still we may stand with bowed head and cry each one, "God be merciful to me a sinner." Still may we cry like sinking Peter, "Lord save, or I perish." Like David, we may be unable to go up to the temple, but we can still go to our God in prayer. The prodigal has lost his substance, but he has not lost his power to supplicate. He has been feeding swine, but as yet he is still a man, and has not lost the faculty of desire and entreaty. He may have forgotten his Father, but his Father has not forgotten him; he may arise and he may go to him, and he may pour out his soul in his Father's bosom. Therefore, let us give thanks unto God that he has nowhere said unto us "Seek ye my face in vain." If we find a desire to pray trembling within our soul, and if though almost extinct we feel some hope in the promise of our gracious God, if our heart still groans after holiness and after God, though she hath lost her power to pray with joyful confidence as once she did, yet let us be thankful that we can pray even if it be but a little. In the will and power to pray there lies the capacity for infinite blessedness: he who hath the key of prayer can open heaven, yea, he hath access to the heart of God; therefore, bless God for prayer.

And then, beloved, beyond the fact of prayer and our power to exercise it, there is a further ground of thanksgiving that we have already received great mercy at God's hands. We are not coming to God to ask favours and receive them for the first time in our lives. Why, blessed be his name, if he never granted me another favour, I have enough for which to thank him as long as I have any being. And this, moreover, is to be recollected, that whatever great things we are about to ask, we cannot possibly be seeking for blessings one-half so great as those which we have already received if we are indeed his children. If thou art a Christian, thou hast life in Christ. Art thou about to ask for meat and raiment? The life is more than these. Thou hast already obtained Christ Jesus to be thine, and he that spared him not will deny thee nothing. Is there, I was about to say, anything to compare with the infinite riches which are already ours in Christ Jesus? Let us perpetually thank our Benefactor for what we have while we make request for something more. Should it not be so? Shall not the abundant utterances of the memory of his great goodness run over into our requests, till our petitions are baptized in gratitude. While we come before God, in one aspect, empty handed to receive of his goodness, on the other hand we should never appear before him empty, but come with the fat of our sacrifices, offering praise and glorifying God.

Furthermore, there is this to be remembered, that when we come before God in the hour of trouble, remembering his great goodness to us in the past, and therefore thanking him, we ought to have faith enough to believe that the present trouble, about which we are praying, is sent in love. You will win with God in prayer if you can look at your trials in this light:—"Lord, I have this thorn in the flesh, I beseech thee, deliver me from it, but meanwhile I bless thee for it; for though I do not understand the why or the wherefore of it, I am persuaded there is love within it; therefore, while I ask thee to remove it, so far as it seemeth evil to me, yet wherein it may to thy better knowledge work my good, I bless thee for it, and I am content to endure it so long as thou seest fit." Is not that a sweet way of praying? "Lord, I am in want, be pleased to supply me; but, meanwhile, if thou do not, I believe it is better for me to be in need, and so I praise thee for my necessity while I ask thee to supply it. I glory in mine infirmity, even while I ask thee to overcome it. I triumph before thee in my affliction, and bless thee for it even while I ask thee to help me in it and to rescue me out of it." This is a royal way of praying: such an amalgam of prayer and thanksgiving is more precious than the gold of Ophir.

Furthermore, beloved, whenever we are on our knees in prayer, it becomes us to bless God that prayer has been answered so many times before. Here thy poor petitioner bends before thee to ask again, but ere he asks he thanks thee for having heard him so many times before. I know that thou hearest me always, therefore do I continue still to cry to thee. My thanksgivings urge me to make fresh petitions, encouraging me in the full confidence that thou wilt not send me away empty. Why, many of the mercies which you possess to-day, and rejoice in, are answers to prayer: they are dear to you because, like Samuel, whom his mother so named because he was "asked of God," they came to you as answers to your supplications. When mercies come in answer to prayer they have a double delight about them, not only because they are good in themselves, but because they are certificates of our favour with the Lord. Well, then, as God has heard us so often and we have the proofs of his hearing, should we ever pray with murmurings and complainings? Should we not rather feel an intense delight when we approach the throne of grace, a rapture awakened by sunny memories of the past?

Again, we ought to pray with thanksgiving in its highest of all senses, by thanking God that we have the mercy which we seek. I wish we could learn this high virtue of faith. When I was conversing lately with our dear friend George Müller, he frequently astonished me with the way in which he mentioned that he had for so many months and years asked for such and such a mercy, and praised the Lord for it. He praised the Lord for it as though he had actually obtained it. Even in praying for the conversion of a person, as soon as he had begun to intercede he began also to praise God for the conversion of that person. Though I think he told us he had in one instance already prayed for thirty years and the work was not yet done, yet all the while he had gone on thanking God, because he knew the prayer would be answered. He believed that he had his petition, and commenced to magnify the Giver of it. Is this unreasonable? How often do we antedate our gratitude among the sons of men! If you were to promise some poor person that you would pay his rent when it came due, he would thank you directly, though not a farthing had left your pocket. We have enough faith in our fellow-men to thank them beforehand, and surely we may do the same with our Lord. Shall we not be willing to trust God for a few months ahead, ay, and for years beforehand, if his wisdom bids us wait. This is the way to win with him. When ye pray believe that ye receive the boons ye ask, and ye shall have them. "Believe that ye have it," says the Scripture, "and ye shall have it." As a man's note of hand stands for the money, so let God's promise be accounted as the performance. Shall not heaven's bank-notes pass as cash? Yea, verily, they shall have unquestioned currency among believers. We will bless the Lord for giving us what we have sought, since our having it is a matter of absolute certainty. We shall never thank God by faith and then find that we were befooled; he has said "All things whatsoever ye shall ask in prayer, believing, ye shall receive." And therefore we may rest assured that the thanksgiving of faith shall never bring shame into the face of the man who offers it.

Once again, and then I will say no more upon these grounds of thanksgiving; surely, brethren, if the Lord do not answer the prayer which we are offering, yet still he is so good, so supremely good, that we will bless him whether or no. We ought even to praise him when he does not answer us, ay, and bless him for refusing our desires. How devoutly might some of us thank him that he did not answer our prayers when we sought for evil things in the ignorance of our childish minds. We asked for flesh, and he might have sent us quails in his anger, and while the flesh was yet in our mouths his wrath might have come upon us; but in love he would not hear us. Blessed be his name for closing his ear in pity! Let us adore him when he keeps us waiting at his doors; thank him for rebuffs, and bless him for refusals, believing always that Ralph Erskine spoke the truth when he said:

"I'm heard when answered soon or late,
Yea, heard when I no answer get;
Yea, kindly answered when refused,
And treated well when harshly used."

Faith glorifies the love of God, for she knows that the Lord's roughest usage is only love in disguise. We are not so sordid as to make our songs depend upon the weather, or on the fulness of the olive-press and the wine-fat. Blessed be his name, he must be right even when he seems at cross purposes with his people; we are not going to quarrel with him, like silly babes with their nurses, because he does not happen to grant us every desire of our foolish hearts. Though he slay us we will trust in him, much more if he decline our requests. We ask him for our daily bread, and if he withhold it we will praise him. Our praises are not suspended upon his answers to our prayers. If the labour of the olive should fail, and the field should yield no fruit; if the flock should be cut off from the fold, and the herd from the stall, yet still would we rejoice in the Lord, and joy in the God of our salvation. Blessed Spirit, raise us to this state of grace and keep us there.

Of that which we have spoken this is the sum: under every condition, and in every necessity, draw nigh to God in prayer, but always bring thanksgiving with you. As Joseph said to his brethren, "Ye shall not see my face unless your younger brother be with you," so may the Lord say to you, "You shall not receive my smile unless you bring thankfulness with you." Let your prayers be like those ancient missals which one sometimes sees, in which the initial letters of the prayers are gilded and adorned with a profusion of colours, the work of cunning writers. Let even the general confession of sin and the Litany of mournful petitions have at least one illuminated letter. Illuminate your prayers; light them up with rays of thanksgiving all the way through; and when you come together to pray forget not to make melody unto the Lord with psalms, and hymns, and spiritual songs.

II. Secondly, I shall drive at the same point, while I try to show THE EVIL OF THE ABSENCE OF THANKSGIVING in our prayers.

First and foremost, we should be chargeable with ingratitude. Are we to be always receiving and never to return thanks? Aristotle rightly observes, "a return is required to preserve friendship between two persons," and as we have nothing else to give to God except gratitude, let us abound therein. If we have no fruit of the field, let us at least render to him the fruit of our lips. Have you no thanks to bring? How, then, can you expect further favours? Does not liberality itself close its hand when ingratitude stands in the way? What, never a word of gratitude to him from whom all blessings flow! Then may even the ungodly despise you.

Next, it would argue great selfishness if we did not combine praise with prayer. Can it be right to think only of ourselves, to pray for benefits and never honour our Benefactor? Are we going to import the detestable vice of avarice into spiritual things, and only care for our own souls' good? What, no thought for God's glory! No idea of magnifying his great and blessed name! God forbid that we should fall into a spirit so mean and narrow. Healthy praise and thanksgiving must be cultivated, because they prevent prayer from becoming overgrown with the mildew of selfishness.

Thanksgiving also prevents prayer from becoming an exhibition of the want of faith; for indeed some prayer is rather a manifestation of the absence of faith than the exercise of confidence in God. If when I am in trouble I still bless the Lord for all I suffer, therein my faith is seen. If before I obtain the mercy I thank God for the grace which I have not yet tasted, therein my faith is manifest. What, is our faith such that it only sings in the sunshine? Have we no nightingale music for our God? Is our trust like the swallow, which must leave us in winter? Is our faith a flower which needs the conservatory to keep it alive? Can it not blossom like the gentian at the foot of the frozen glacier, where the damp and chill of adversity surround it? I trust it can, it ought to do so, and we ought to feel that we can praise and bless God when outward circumstances appear rather to demand sighs than songs.

Not to thank God in our prayers would argue wilfulness, and want of submission to his will. Must everything be ordered according to our mind? To refuse to praise unless we have our own way is great presumption, and shows that like a naughty child we will sulk if we cannot be master. I might illustrate the wilfulness of many a supplication by that of a little boy who was very diligent in saying his prayers, but was at the same time disobedient, ill-tempered, and the pest of the house. His mother told him that she thought it was mere hypocrisy for him to pretend to pray. He replied, "No, mother, indeed it is not, for I pray God to lead you and father to like my ways better than you do." Numbers of people want the Lord to like their ways better, but they do not intend to follow the ways of the Lord. Their minds are contrary to God and will not submit to his will, and therefore there is no thanksgiving in them. Praise in a prayer is indicative of a humble, submissive, obedient spirit, and when it is absent we may suspect wilfulness and self-seeking. Very much of the prayer of rebellious hearts is the mere growling of an angry obstinacy, the whine of an ungratified self-conceit. God must do this and he must do that, or else we will not love him. What baby talk! What spoiled children such are! A little whipping will do them good. "I have never believed in the goodness of God," said one, "ever since he took my dear mother away." I knew a good man whose child was on the verge of the grave; when I went to see her he charged me not to mention death to her, for he said, "I do not believe God could do such an unkind action as take my only child away." When I assured him that she would surely die within a few days, and that he must not quarrel with the will of the Lord, he stood firm in his rebellion. He prayed, but he could not bless God, and it was no marvel that his heart sank within him, and he refused to be comforted, when at last his child died, as we all felt sure she would. He became afterwards resigned, but his want of acquiescence cost him many a smart. This will not do; this quarrelling with God is poor work! Resignation comes to the heart like an angel unawares, and when we entertain it our soul is comforted. We may ask for the child's life, but we must also thank the Lord that the dear life has been prolonged so long as it has been, and we must put the child and everything else into our Father's hands and say, "If thou shouldest take all away, yet still will I bless thy name, O thou Most High." This is acceptable prayer, because it is not soured by the leaven of self-will, but salted with thankfulness.

We must mingle our thanksgivings with our prayers, or else we may fear that our mind is not in harmony with the divine will. Recollect, dear friends, that prayer does not alter the mind of God: it never was the intent of prayer that it should attempt anything of the kind. Prayer is the shadow of the decrees of the Eternal. God has willed such a thing, and he makes his saints to will it, and express their will in prayer. Prayer is the rustling of the wings of the angels who are bringing the blessing to us. It is written, "Delight thyself in the Lord and he will give thee the desire of thine heart." It is not said that he will give the desire of his heart to every Jack and Tom, but you must first delight in the Lord, and when your mind finds all her joy in God then it is clear that God and you, as far as it can be, are standing on the same plane and moving in the same direction, and now you shall have the desire of your heart because the desire of your heart is the desire of God's heart. Character, as much as faith, lies at the basis of prevalence in prayer. I do not mean in the case of the prayer of the sinner when he is seeking mercy, but I mean in the habitual prayers of the godly. There are some men who cannot pray so as to prevail, for sin has made them weak, and God walks contrary to them because they walk contrary to him. He who has lost the light of God's countenance has also lost much of the prevalence of his prayers. You do not suppose that every Israelite could have gone to the top of Carmel and opened the windows of heaven as Elijah did. No, he must first be Elijah, for it is the effectual, fervent prayer, not of every man, but of a righteous man, that availeth much; and when the Lord has put your heart and my heart into an agreement with him then we shall pray and prevail. What did our Lord say—"If ye abide in me, and my words abide in you, ye shall ask what ye will, and it shall be done unto you." Doubtless many lose power in prayer because their lives are grievous in the sight of the Lord, and he cannot smile upon them. Will any father listen to the requests of a child who has set himself up in opposition to parental authority? The obedient, tender, loving child, who would not wish for anything which you did not think right to give, is he whose requests you are pleased to consider and fulfil; yea, more, you even anticipate the wishes of such a child, and before he calls you answer him. May we be such children of the great God.

III. And now, in the third place, let us consider THE RESULT OF THE PRESENCE OF THIS THANKSGIVING IN CONNECTION WITH PRAYER. According to the context, the presence of thanksgiving in the heart together with prayer is productive of peace. "In everything by prayer and supplication with thanksgiving let your requests be made known unto God, and the peace of God, which passeth all understanding, shall keep your hearts and minds through Christ Jesus." Now that peace, that conscious calm, that divine serenity, which is described as the peace of God, is not produced by prayer alone, but by prayer with thanksgiving. Some men pray, and therein they do well; but for lack of mixing thanksgiving with it their prayer agitates them, and they come away from the closet even more anxious than when they entered it. If they mingled in their petitions that sweet powder of the merchants, which is called praise, and mixed it after the art of the apothecary, in due proportions, the blessing of God would come with it, causing repose of heart. If we bless our gracious Lord for the very trouble we pray against; if we bless him for the very mercy which we need, as though it had already come; if we resolve to praise him whether we receive the boon or not, learning in whatsoever state we are therewith to be content, then "the peace of God, which passeth all understanding, will keep our hearts and minds by Christ Jesus." Brethren, as you value this divine rest of spirit, as you prize constant serenity of soul, I beseech you mingle praises with your prayers.

The next effect of it will be this: the thanksgiving will often warm the soul, and enable it to pray. I believe it is the experience of many who love secret devotion that at times they cannot pray, for their heart seems hard, cold, dumb, and almost dead. Do not pump up unwilling and formal prayer, my brethren; but take down the hymn-book and sing. While you praise the Lord for what you have, you will find your rocky heart begin to dissolve and flow in rivers. You will be encouraged to plead with the Lord because you will remember what you have aforetime received at his hand. If you had an empty waggon to raise to the mouth of a coal-pit, it might be a very difficult task for you; but the work is managed easily by the common-sense of the miners. They make the full waggons as they run down pull the empty waggons up the incline. Now, when your heart is loaded with praise for mercy received let it run down the incline, and draw up the empty waggon of your desires, and you will thus find it easy to pray. Cold and chill prayers are always to be deplored, and if by so simple a method as entreating the Lord to accept our thanksgiving our hearts can be warmed and renewed, let us by all means take care to use it.

Lastly, I believe that when a man begins to pray with thanksgiving he is upon the eve of receiving the blessing. God's time to bless you has come when you begin to praise him as well as pray to him. God has his set time to favour us, and he will not grant us our desire until the due season has arrived. But the time has come when you begin to bless the Lord. Now, take an instance of this in the second Book of Chronicles, twentieth chapter and twentieth verse. Jehoshaphat went out to fight with an exceeding great army, and mark how he achieved the victory. "They rose early in the morning and went forth into the wilderness of Tekoa: and as they went forth, Jehoshaphat stood and said, Hear me, O Judah, and ye inhabitants of Jerusalem; believe in the Lord your God, so shall ye be established; believe his prophets, so shall ye prosper. And when he had consulted with the people he appointed"—what? warriors, captains? No, that was all done, but he "appointed singers unto the Lord, and that should praise the beauty of holiness, as they went out before the army, and to say, Praise the Lord; for his mercy endureth for ever. And when they began to sing and to praise, the Lord set ambushments against the children of Ammon, Moab, and mount Seir, which were come against Judah; and they were smitten." Victory came when they began to sing and to praise. You shall get your answers to prayer when you multiply your thanksgivings in all your prayers and supplications: rest you sure of that.

Our thanksgiving will show that the reason for our waiting is now exhausted; that the waiting has answered its purpose, and may now come to a joyful end. Sometimes we are not in a fit state to receive a blessing, but when we reach the condition of thankfulness then is the time when it is safe for God to indulge us. A professing Christian came to his minister once and said, "Sir, you say we should always pray." "Yes, my friend, undoubtedly." "But then, Sir, I have been praying for twelve months that I might enjoy the comforts of religion, and I am no happier than before. I have made that my one perpetual prayer, that I might enjoy the comforts of religion, and I do not feel joy nor even peace of mind; in fact, I have more doubts and fears than ever I had." "Yes," said his minister, "and that is the natural result of such a selfish prayer. Why, dear friend," he said, "come and kneel down with me, and let us pray in another manner, 'Father, glorify thy name! Thy kingdom come.' Now," said he, "go and offer those petitions and get to work to try to make it true, and see if you do not soon enjoy the comforts of religion." There is a great deal in that fact: if you will but desire God to be glorified, and aim at glorifying him yourself, then shall the joys of true godliness come to you in answer to prayer.

The time for the blessing is when you begin to praise God for it. For, brethren, you may be sure that when you put up a thanksgiving on the ground that

God has answered your prayer, you really have prevailed with God. Suppose you had promised to some poor woman that you would give her a meal to-morrow. You might forget it, you know; but suppose when the morning came she sent her little girl with a basket for it, she would be likely to get it I think. But, suppose that she sent in addition a little note in which the poor soul thanked you for your great kindness, could you have the heart to say, "My dear girl, I cannot attend to you to-day. Come another time"? Oh dear no, if the cupboard was bare you would send out to get something, because the good soul so believed in you that she had sent you thanks for it before she received your gift. Well, now, trust the Lord in the same manner. He cannot run back from his word, my brethren. Believing prayer holds him, but believing thanksgiving binds him. If it is not in your own heart, though you be evil, to refuse to give what you have promised when that promise is so believed that the person rejoices as though he had it; then depend upon it the good God will not find it in his heart to refuse. The time for reception is fully come because thanksgiving for that reception fills your heart. I leave the matter with you. If you are enabled to pray in that fashion, great good will come to yourselves, and to the Church of God, and to the world at large by such prayers.

Now, I think I hear in this audience somebody saying, "But I cannot pray so. I do not know how to pray. Oh, that I knew how to pray! I am a poor, guilty sinner. I cannot mix any thanksgiving with my supplications." Ah, my dear soul, do not think about that just now. I am not so much preaching to you as I am preaching to the people of God. For you it is quite enough to say, "God be merciful to me a sinner." And yet I will venture to say that there is praise in such a petition. You are implicitly praising the justice of God, and you are praising his mercy by appealing to him. When the prodigal returned, and he began his prayer by saying, "I am not worthy to be called thy son," there was in that confession a real praise of the father's goodness, of which he was unworthy to partake. But you need not think about this matter at present, for just you have to find Jesus, and eternal life in him. Go and plead the merit of Jesus, and cast yourself upon the love and mercy of God in him, and he will not cast you away: and then another day, when you thus have found and known him, take care that the thanksgiving for your salvation never ceases. Even when you are most hungry, and poor, and needy in the future continue to bless your saving Lord, and say, "This poor man cried, and the Lord heard him: and because the Lord inclined his ear unto me I will praise his name as long as I live."

God bless you, for Jesus' sake. Amen.

9
PRAY WITHOUT CEASING

"Pray without ceasing."—*1 Thessalonians 5:17*

"As we breathe without ceasing, so must we pray without ceasing."

~

THE position of our text is very suggestive. Observe what it follows. It comes immediately after the precept, "Rejoice evermore;" as if that command had somewhat staggered the reader, and made him ask, "How can I always rejoice?" and, therefore, the apostle appended as answer, "Always pray." The more praying the more rejoicing. Prayer gives a channel to the pent-up sorrows of the soul, they flow away, and in their stead streams of sacred delight pour into the heart. At the same time the more rejoicing the more praying; when the heart is in a quiet condition, and full of joy in the Lord, then also will it be sure to draw nigh unto the Lord in worship. Holy joy and prayer act and react upon each other.

Observe, however, what immediately follows the text: "In everything give thanks." When joy and prayer are married their first born child is gratitude. When we joy in God for what we have, and believingly pray to him for more, then our souls thank him both in the enjoyment of what we have, and in the prospect of what is yet to come. Those three texts are three companion pictures, representing the life of a true Christian, the central sketch is the connecting link between those on either side. These three precepts are an ornament of grace to every believer's neck, wear them every one of you, for glory and for beauty. "Rejoice evermore;" "pray without ceasing;" "in everything give thanks."

But we cannot spare any time for the consideration of the context, but must advance to the precept in hand. Our text though exceedingly short is marvellously full, and we will discuss it under the following heads. We shall ask and answer four questions. *What do these words imply?* Secondly, *What do they actually mean?* Thirdly, *How shall we obey them?* And, fourthly, *Why should* WE *especially obey them?*

I. WHAT DO THESE WORDS IMPLY? "Pray without ceasing." Do they not imply that *the use of the voice is not an essential element in prayer?* It would be most unseemly even if it were possible for us to continue unceasingly to pray aloud. There would of course be no opportunity for preaching and hearing, for the exchange of friendly intercourse, for business, or for any other of the duties of life; while the din of so many voices would remind our neighbours rather of the worship of Baal than that of Zion. It was never the design of the Lord Jesus that our throats, lungs, and tongues should be for ever at work. Since we are to pray without ceasing, and yet could not pray with the voice without ceasing, it is clear that audible language is not essential to prayer. We may speak a thousand words which seem to be prayer, and yet never pray; on the other hand, we may cry into God's ear most effectually, and yet never say a word. In the book of Exodus God is represented as saying to Moses, "Why criest thou unto me?" And yet it is not recorded that Moses had uttered so much as a single syllable at that time. It is true that the use of the voice often helps prayer. I find, personally, that I can pray best when alone if I can hear my own voice; at the same time it is not essential, it does not enter at all into the acceptability, reality, or prevalence of prayer. Silence is as fit a garment for devotion as any that language can fashion.

It is equally clear that *the posture of prayer is of no great importance*, for if it were necessary that we should pray on our knees we could not pray without ceasing, the posture would become painful and injurious. To what end has our Creator given us feet, if he desires us never to stand upon them? If he had meant us to be on our knees without ceasing, he would have fashioned the body differently, and would not have endowed us with such unnecessary length of limb. It is well to pray on one's knees; it is a most fitting posture; it is one which expresses humility, and when humility is truly felt, kneeling is a natural and beautiful token of it, but, at the same time, good men have prayed flat upon their faces, have prayed sitting, have prayed standing, have prayed in any posture, and the posture does not enter into the essence of prayer. Consent not to be placed in bondage by those to whom the bended knee is reckoned of more importance than the contrite heart.

It is clear, too, from the text, that *the place is not*

essential to prayer, for if there were only certain holy places where prayer was acceptable, and we had to pray without ceasing, our churches ought to be extremely large, that we might always live in them, and they would have to comprise all the arrangements necessary for human habitations. If it be true that there is some sanctity this side of a brick-wall more than there is on the other side of it, if it be true that the fresh air blows away grace, and that for the highest acceptance we need groined arches, pillars, aisle, chancel, and transept, then farewell, ye green lanes, and fair gardens, and lovely woods, for henceforth we must, without ceasing, dwell where your fragrance and freshness can never reach us. But this is ridiculous; wherefore I gather that the frequenting of some one particular place has little or nothing to do with prayer; and such a conclusion is consistent with the saying of Paul upon Mars' Hill, "God that made the world and all things therein, seeing that he is Lord of heaven and earth, dwelleth not in temples made with hands."

"Pray without ceasing." That precept at one stroke *overthrows the idea of particular times* wherein prayer is more acceptable or more proper than at others. If I am to pray without ceasing, then every second must be suitable for prayer, and there is not one unholy moment in the hour, nor one unaccepted hour in the day, nor one unhallowed day in the year. The Lord has not appointed a certain week for prayer, but all weeks should be weeks of prayer: neither has he said that one hour of the day is more acceptable than another. All time is equally legitimate for supplication, equally holy, equally accepted with God, or else we should not have been told to pray without ceasing. It is good to have your times of prayer; it is good to set apart seasons for special supplication—we have no doubt of that; but we must never allow this to gender the superstition that there is a certain holy hour for prayer in the morning, a specially acceptable hour for prayer in the evening, and a sacred time for prayer at certain seasons of the year. Wherever we seek the Lord with true hearts he is found of us; whenever we cry unto him he heareth us. Every place is hallowed ground to a hallowed heart, and every day is a holy day to a holy man. From January to December the calendar has not one date in which prayer is forbidden. All the days are red-letter days, whether Sabbaths or week days they are all accepted times for prayer. Clear, then, is it from the text, that the voice, the posture, the place, the time—none of them enter into the essence of prayer, or else, in this case, we should be commanded to perform an impossibility, which we are quite certain is not after the manner of the Lord our God.

There is one other thing implied in the text, namely, that *a Christian has no right to go into any place where he could not continue to pray.* Pray without ceasing? Then I am never to be in a place where I could not pray without ceasing. Hence, many worldly amusements without being particularised may be judged and condemned at once. Certain people believe in ready-made prayers, cut and dried for all occasions, and, at the same time, they believe persons to be regenerated in baptism though their lives are anything but Christian; ought they not to provide prayers for all circumstances in which these, the dear regenerated but graceless sons and daughters of their church, are found? As, for instance, a pious collect for a young prince or nobleman, who is about to go to a shooting-match, that he may be forgiven for his cruelty towards those poor pigeons who are only badly wounded and made to linger in misery, as also a prayer for a religious and regenerated gentleman who is going to a horserace, and a collect for young persons who have received the grace of confirmation, upon their going to the theatre to attend a very questionable play. Could not such special collects be made to order? You revolt at the idea. Well, then, have nothing to do with that which you cannot ask God's blessing upon, have nothing to do with it, for if God cannot bless it, you may depend upon it the devil has cursed it. Anything that is right for you to do you may consecrate with prayer, and let this be a sure gauge and test to you, if you feel that it would be an insult to the majesty of heaven for you to ask the Lord's blessing upon what is proposed to you, then stand clear of the unholy thing. If God doth not approve, neither must you have fellowship therewith.

These matters are clearly implied in the precept, "Pray without ceasing."

II. But now, WHAT DOES THIS ACTUALLY MEAN? If it does not mean we are to be always on our knees, nor always saying prayers, nor always in church or in meeting, and does not mean that we are to consider any day as unfit for praying, what then? The words mean, first, *a privilege;* secondly, *a precept*—"Pray without ceasing." Our Lord Jesus Christ in these words assures you that you may pray without ceasing. There is no time when you may not pray. You have here permission given to come to the mercy-seat when you will, for the veil of the Most Holy place is rent in twain from the top to the bottom, and our access to the mercy-seat is undisputed and indisputable. Kings hold their levees upon certain appointed days, and then their courtiers are admitted; but the King of kings holds a constant levee. The monarch whose palace was in Shushan would have none approach him unless he sent for them; but the King of kings has called for all his people, and they may come at all times. They were slain who went in unto the king Ahasuerus, unless he stretched out his sceptre to them; but our King never withdraws his sceptre, it is always stretched out, and whosoever desires to come to him may come now, and come at any time. Among the Persians there were some few of the nobility who had the peculiar and special right of an audience with the king at any time they chose. Now, that which was the peculiar right of a very few and of the very great is the privilege of every child of God. He may come in unto the King at all times. The dead of night is not too late for God; the breaking of the morning, when the first grey light is seen, is not too early for the Most High; at midday he is not too busy; and when the evening gathers he is not weary with his children's prayers. "Pray without ceasing," is, if I read it aright, a most sweet and precious permit to the believer to pour out his heart at all times before the Lord. I hear its still small voice saying, "Come to the mercy seat, O my child, whenever thou wilt; come to the treasury of grace whenever thou desirest—

> The happy gates of gospel grace
> Stand open night and day."

The doors of the temple of divine love shall not be shut. Nothing can set a barrier between a praying soul and its God. The road of angels and of prayers is ever open. Let us but send out the dove of prayer and we may be certain that she will return unto us with an olive branch of peace in her mouth. Evermore the Lord hath regard unto the pleadings of his servants, and waiteth to be gracious unto them.

Still, however, it is *a precept*, "Pray without ceasing." And what does it mean? It means a great truth which I cannot very well convey to you in a few words, and, therefore, must try and bring out under four or five points.

It means, first, *never abandon prayer*. Never for any cause or reason cease to pray. Imagine not that you must pray until you are saved, and may then leave off. For those whose sins are pardoned prayer is quite as needful as for those mourning under a sense of sin. "Pray without ceasing," for in order that you may persevere in grace you must persevere in prayer. Should you become experienced in grace and enriched with much spiritual knowledge, you must not dream of restraining prayer because of your gifts and graces. "Pray without ceasing," or else your flower will fade and your spiritual fruit will never ripen. Continue in prayer until the last moment of your life.

> "Long as they live must Christians pray,
> For only while they pray they live."

As we breathe without ceasing, so must we pray without ceasing. As there is no attainment in life, of health, or of strength, or of muscular vigour which can place a man beyond the necessity of breathing, so no condition of spiritual growth or advance in grace will allow a man to dispense with prayer.

"Let us pray! our life is praying;
    Prayer with time alone may cease:
Then in heaven, God's will obeying,
    Life is praise and perfect peace."

Never give up praying, not even though Satan should suggest to you that it is in vain for you to cry unto God. Pray in his teeth; "pray without ceasing." If for awhile the heavens are as brass and your prayer only echoes in thunder above your head, pray on; if month after month your prayer appears to have miscarried, and no reply has been vouchsafed to you, yet still continue to draw nigh unto the Lord. Do not abandon the mercy-seat for any reason whatever. If it be a good thing that you have been asking for, and you are sure it is according to the divine will, if the vision tarry wait for it, pray, weep, entreat, wrestle, agonise till you get that which you are praying for. If your heart be cold in prayer, do not restrain prayer until your heart warms, but pray your soul unto heat by the help of the ever-blessed Spirit who helpeth our infirmities. If the iron be hot then hammer it, and if it be cold hammer it till you heat it. Never cease prayer for any sort of reason or argument. If the philosopher should tell you that every event is fixed, and, therefore, prayer cannot possibly change anything, and, consequently, must be folly; still, if you cannot answer him and are somewhat puzzled, go on with your supplications notwithstanding all. No difficult problem concerning digestion would prevent your eating, for the result justifies the practice, and so no quibble should make us cease prayer, for the assured success of it commends it to us. You know what your God has told you, and if you cannot reply to every difficulty which man can suggest, resolve to be obedient to the divine will, and still "Pray without ceasing." Never, never, never renounce the habit of prayer, or your confidence in its power.

A second meaning is this. *Never suspend the regular offering of prayer.* You will, if you are a watchful Christian, have your times of daily devotion, fixed not by superstition, but for your convenience and remembrance; just as David, three times a day, and as another saint, seven times a day, sought the Lord: now be sure to keep up this daily prayer without intermission. This advice will not comprehend the whole range of the text, I am not pretending that it does; I am only mentioning it now as supplementary to other thoughts. "Pray without ceasing;" that is, never give up the morning prayer, nor the evening prayer, nor the prayer at midday if such has grown to be your habit. If you change the hours and times, as you may, yet keep up the practice of regularly recurring retirement, meditation, and prayer. You may be said to continue in prayer if your habitual devotions be maintained. It would be quite correct for me to say that I know a man who has been always begging ever since I have been in London. I do not think that I ever passed the spot where he stands without seeing him there. He is a blind person, and stands near a church. As long as my recollection serves me he has been begging without ceasing; of course he has not begged when he has been asleep, he has not begged when he has gone home to his meals, nor did you understand me to have asserted anything so absurd when I said he had begged without ceasing for years. And so, if at those times when it is proper for you to separate yourself from your ordinary labours, you continue perseveringly begging at mercy's throne, it may be with comparative correctness said of you that you pray without ceasing. Though all hours are alike to me, I find it profitable to meet with God at set periods, for these seem to me to be like the winding up of the clock. The clock is to go all day, but there is a time for winding it up; and the little special season that we set apart and hedge round about for communion with our God, seems to wind us up for the rest of the day. Therefore, if you would pray without ceasing, continue in the offering of the morning and the evening sacrifice, and let it be perpetually an ordinance with you, that your times of prayer are not broken in upon.

That, however, is only a help, for I must add, thirdly, *between these times of devotion, labour to be much in ejaculatory prayer*. While your hands are busy with the world, let your hearts still talk with God; not in twenty sentences at a time, for such an interval might be inconsistent with your calling, but in broken sentences and interjections. It is always wrong to present one duty to God stained with the blood of another, and that we should do if we spoiled study or labour by running away to pray at all hours; but we may, without this, let short sentences go up to heaven, ay, and we may shoot upwards cries, and single words, such as an "Ah," an "Oh," an "O that;" or, without words we may pray in the upward glancing of the eye or the sigh of the heart. He who prays without ceasing uses many little darts and hand-grenades of godly desire, which he casts forth at every available interval. Sometimes he will blow the furnace of his desires to a great heat in regular prayer, and as a consequence at other times, the sparks will continue to rise up to heaven in the form of brief words, and looks, and desires.

Fourthly, if we would pray without ceasing, *we must be always in the spirit of prayer.* Our heart, renewed by the Holy Ghost, must be like the magnetised needle, which always has an inclination towards the pole. It does not always point to that pole, you can turn it aside if you will; in an iron ship it exhibits serious deflections, under all circumstances it is not exactly true; but if you put your finger to that needle and force it round to the east, you have only to take away the pressure, and immediately it returns to its beloved pole again. So let your heart be magnetised with prayer, so that if the finger of duty turns it away from the immediate act of prayer, there may still be the longing desire for prayer in your soul, and the moment you can do so, your heart reverts to its beloved work. As perfume lies in flowers even when they do not shed their fragrance upon the gale, so let prayer lie in your hearts.

But, perhaps, the last meaning that I shall give has the most of the truth of the text in it, namely this: *Let all your actions be consistent with your prayers, and be in fact a continuation of your prayers.* If I am to pray without ceasing, it cannot mean that I am always to be in the act of direct devotion; for the human mind, as at present constituted, needs variety of occupation, and it could not without producing madness or imbecility continue always in the exercise of one function. We must, therefore, change the *modus* or the manner of operation if we are ceaselessly to continue in prayer. We must pursue our prayers, but do it in another manner. Take an instance. This morning I prayed to God to arouse his people to prayerfulness; very well;

as I came to this house my soul continued to ejaculate, "O Lord, awaken thy children to prayerfulness." Now, while I am preaching to you and driving at the same point, am I not praying? Is not my sermon the continuation of my prayer, for I am desiring and aiming at the same thing? Is it not a continuing to pray when we use the best means towards the obtaining of that which we pray for? Do you not see my point? He who prays for his fellow creatures, and then seeks their good, is praying still. In this sense there is truth in that old distich.

"He prayeth best that loveth best,
Both man, and bird, and beast."

Loving is praying. If I seek in prayer the good of my fellow creature, and then go and try to promote it, I am practically praying for his good in my actions. If I seek, as I should do, God's glory above everything, then if all my actions are meant to tend to God's glory, I am continuing to pray, though I may not be praying with my thoughts or with my lips. Oh, that our whole life might be a prayer. It can be. There can be a praying without ceasing before the Lord, though there be many pausings in what the most of men would call prayer. Pray then without ceasing, my brother. Let thy whole life be praying. If thou changest the method, yet change not the pursuit; but continue still to worship, still to adore. This I think to be the meaning of our text,—never altogether abandon prayer; do not suspend the regular offering of prayer; be much in earnest ejaculations, be always in the spirit of prayer, and let the whole of your life be consistent with your prayer, and become a part of it.

III. HOW CAN WE OBEY THESE WORDS? First, let

us labour as much as we can to prevent all *sinful* interruptions. "Pray without ceasing." Then if it be impossible to be in the act of prayer always, at least let us be as much as possible in that act; and let us prevent those interruptions which I mentioned in the early part of my discourse, the interruptions occasioned by our own sin. Let us endeavour to keep clear, as far as we can, of anything and everything in ourselves, or round about us, that would prevent our abounding in supplication. And let us also keep clear of interruptions from the sins of others. Do others forbid us to pray? Let us not be afraid of their wrath. Remember Daniel, who while he was under the penalty of being cast into a den of lions, yet opened his window towards Jerusalem, and prayed seven times a day as he had done aforetime. Under no threats and for no bribes, let us ever cease to pray. In private let us always pray, and if duty calls us to do so where others observe us, let us so much fear the eye of God that we shall not dare to fear the eye of man.

Let us next avoid all *unnecessary* interruptions of every sort to our prayer. If we know that any matter, from which we can escape, has a tendency to disturb the spirit of prayer within us, let us avoid it earnestly. Let us try, as much as possible, not to be put off the scent in prayer. Satan's object will be to distract the mind, to throw it off the rails, to divert its aim, but let us resolve before God, we will not turn aside from following hard after him. Sir Thomas Abney had for many years practised family prayer regularly; he was elected Lord Mayor of London, and on the night of his election he must be present at a banquet, but when the time came for him to call his family together in prayer, having no wish either to be a Pharisee or to give up his practice, he excused himself to the guests in this way,—he said he had an important engagement with a very dear friend, and they must excuse him for a few minutes. It was most true, his dearest friend was the Lord Jesus, and family prayer was an important engagement; and so he withdrew for awhile to the family altar, and in that respect prayed without ceasing. We sometimes allow good things to interrupt our prayer, and thus make them evil. Mrs. Rowe observes in one of her letters, that if the twelve apostles were preaching in the town were she lived, and she could never hear them again, if it were her time for private devotion, she would not be bribed out of her closet by the hope of hearing them. I am not sure but what she might have taken another time for her private devotions, and so have enjoyed both privileges, but at the same time, supposing she must have lost the prayer and have only got the preaching in exchange, I agree with her, it would have been exchanging gold for silver. She would be more profited in praying than she would be in hearing, for praying is the end of preaching. Preaching is but the wheat-stalk, but praying is the golden grain itself, and he hath the best who gets it.

Sometimes we think we are too busy to pray. That also is a great mistake, for praying is a saving of time. You remember Luther's remark, "I have so much to do to-day that I shall never get through it with less than three hours' prayer." He had not been accustomed to take so much time for pray on ordinary days, but since that was a busy day, he must needs have more communion with his God. But, perhaps, our occupations begin early, and we therefore say, "How can I get alone with God in prayer?" It is said of Sir Henry Havelock that every morning when the march began at six, he always rose at four, that he might not miss his time for the reading of the Scripture and communion with his God. If we have no time we must make time, for if God has given us time for secondary duties, he must have given us time for primary ones, and to draw near to him is a primary duty, and we must let nothing set it on one side. There is no real need to sacrifice any duty, we have time enough for all if we are not idle; and, indeed, the one will help the other instead of clashing with it. When Edward Payson was a student at College, he found he had so much to do to attend his classes and prepare for examinations, that he could not spend as much time as he should in private prayer; but, at last, waking up to the feeling that he was going back in divine things through his habits, he took due time for devotion, and he asserts in his diary that he did more in his studies in a single week after he had spent time with God in prayer, than he had accomplished in twelve months before. God can multiply our ability to make use of time. If we give the Lord his due, we shall have enough for all necessary purposes. In this matter seek first the kingdom of God and his righteousness, and all these things shall be added to you. Your other engagements will run smoothly if you do not forget your engagement with God.

We must, dear friends, in order to pray without ceasing, strive against *indolence* in prayer. I believe that no man loves prayer until the Holy Spirit has taught him the sweetness and value of it. If you have ever prayed without ceasing you will pray without ceasing. The men who do not love to pray must be strangers to its secret joy. When prayer is a mechanical act, and there is no soul in it, it is a slavery and a weariness; but when it is really living prayer, and when the man prays because he is a Christian and cannot help praying, when he prays along the street, prays in his business, prays in the house, prays in the field, when his whole soul is full of prayer, then he cannot have too much of it. He will not be backward in prayer who meets Jesus in it, but he who knows not the Well-beloved will count it a drudgery.

Let us avoid, above all things, *lethargy and indifference* in prayer. Oh, it is a dreadful thing that ever we should insult the majesty of heaven by words from which our heart has gone. I must, my spirit, I must school thee to this, that thou must have communion with God, and if in thy prayer thou dost not talk with God, thou shalt keep on praying till thou dost. Come not away from the mercy-seat till thou hast prayed.

Beloved brother, say unto thy soul, thus—"here have I come to the throne of grace to worship God and seek his blessing, and I am not going away till I have done this; I will not rise from my knees, because I have spent my customary minutes, but here will I pray till I find the blessing." Satan will often leave off tempting when he finds you thus resolute in prayer. Brethren, we need waking up. Routine grows upon us. We get into the mill-horse way—round, and round, and round the mill. From this may God save us. It is deadly. A man may pray twenty years with regularity, as far as the time goes, and the form goes, and never have prayed a single grain of prayer in the whole period. One real groan fetched from the heart is worth a million litanies, one living breath from a gracious soul is worth ten thousand collects. May we be kept awake by God's grace, praying without ceasing.

And we must take care, dear brethren, again, if we would perform this duty, that we fight against anything like *despair* of being heard. If we have not been heard after six times we must, as Elijah, go again seven times; if our Peter is in prison, and the church has prayed God to liberate him, and he still is in fetters bound in the inner prison, let us pray on, for one of these days Peter will knock at the gate. Be importunate, heaven's gate does not open to every runaway knock. Knock, and knock, and knock again; and add to thy knocking asking, and to thy asking seeking, and be not satisfied till thou gettest a real answer.

Never cease from prayer through *presumption;* guard against that. Feel, O Christian, that you always need to pray. Say not, "I *am rich* and increased in goods, and have need of nothing." Thou art by nature still naked, and poor, and miserable; therefore, persevere in prayer, and buy of the Lord fine gold, and clean raiment, that thou mayst be rich, and fitly clothed.

Thus I have tried to set before you, beloved, how by resisting presumption and despair, indolence and lethargy, and trying to put aside all sinful and other interruptions, we may pray without ceasing.

IV. Now, very briefly, in the last place, WHY SHOULD WE OBEY THIS PRECEPT? Of course we should obey it because it is of divine authority; but, moreover, we should attend to it because *the Lord always deserves to be worshipped.* Prayer is a method of worship; continue, therefore, always to render to your Creator, your Preserver, your Redeemer, your Father, the homage of your prayers. With such a King let us not be slack in homage. Let us pay him the revenue of praise continually. Evermore may we magnify and bless his name. His enemies curse him; let us bless him without ceasing. Moreover, brethren, the spirit of love within us surely prompts us to draw near to God without ceasing. Christ is our husband. Is the bride true to her marriage vows if she cares not for her beloved's company? God is our Father. What sort of a child is that which does not desire to climb its father's knee and receive a smile from its father's face? If you and I can live day after day and week after week without anything like communion with God, how dwelleth the love of God in us? "Pray without ceasing," because the Lord never ceases to love you, never ceases to bless you, and never ceases to regard you as his child.

"Pray without ceasing," for you *want a blessing* on all the work you are doing. Is it common work? "Except the Lord build the house, they labour in vain that build it." Is it business? It is vain to rise up early and sit up late, and eat the bread of carefulness, for without God you cannot prosper. You are taught to say, "Give us this day our daily bread,"—an inspired prayer for secular things. Oh, consecrate your seculars by prayer. And, if you are engaged in God's service, what work is there in which you can hope for success without his blessing? To teach the young, to preach the gospel, to distribute tracts, to instruct the ignorant, do not all these want his blessing? What are they if that favour be denied? Pray, therefore, as long as you work.

You are always in *danger of being tempted;* there is no position in life in which you may not be assaulted by the enemy. "Pray without ceasing," therefore. A man who is going along a dark road where he knows that there are enemies, if he must be alone and has a sword with him, he carries it drawn in his hand, to let the robbers know that he he is ready for them. So Christian, pray without ceasing; carry your sword in your hand, wave that mighty weapon of all-prayer of which Bunyan speaks. Never sheathe it; it will cut through coats of mail. You need fear no foe if you can but pray. As you are tempted without ceasing, so pray without ceasing.

You need always to pray, for you *always want* something. In no condition are you so rich as not to need something from your God. It is not possible for you to say, "I have all things;" or, if you can, you have them only in Christ, and from Christ you must continue to seek them. As you are always in need, so beg always at mercy's gate. Moreover, blessings are always waiting for you. Angels are ready with favours that you know not of, and you have but to ask and have. Oh, could you see what might be had for the asking you would not be so slack. The priceless benisons of heaven which lie on one side as yet, oh, did you but, perceive that they are only waiting for you to pray, you would not hesitate a moment. The man who knows that his farming is profitable, and that his land brings forth abundantly, will be glad to sow a broader stretch of land another year; and he who knows that God answers prayer, and is ready still to answer it, will open his mouth yet wider that God may fill it.

Continue to pray, brethren, for even if you should not want prayer yourself there are *others who do*—there are the dying, the sick, the poor, the ignorant, the backsliding, the blaspheming, the heathen at home, and the heathen abroad. "Pray without ceasing," for the enemy works incessantly, and as yet the kingdom has not come unto Zion. You shall never be able to say, "I left off praying, for I had nothing to pray for." This side heaven objects for prayer are as multitudinous as the stars of the sky.

And, now, I said I would say a word as to why WE ought to pray especially, and that shall close the sermon. Beloved friends, this church ought to pray without ceasing. We have been in years past notable for prayer. If ever a church has prayed it has been this church. I might find many faults with some who hinder prayer, but yet I must say in God's sight I know and feel that there has been living prayer in this church for many years, and hence it is we have had many years of peace and prosperity. We have lacked nothing because we have not lacked prayer. I do not doubt we might have had much more if we had prayed more; still prayer has been very mighty here. Now, brethren, suppose you had no pastor, suppose the preacher was gone from you, and that the black cloth upon this pulpit was not for a deceased elder of the church but for the preacher himself, you would pray, would you not? Will you not pray for me then while I live? If you would pray for another to come, will you not pray for me while I am here? I desire to discharge my office before you in God's sight with all earnestness, but I cannot without your prayers, and as being gone from you, you would lift up many sighs, and you would with prayers ask for a successor, pray for me while I am yet with you. Beloved, you have prayed very earnestly for the pastor when he has been sick, your prayers have been his consolation and his restoration; will you not pray for him now that he is able to preach the gospel, that his health may be sanctified to God's service, and the ministry of the truth may be mighty in the winning of souls. I ask it of you, I think I might claim it of you. I do beseech you, brethren, pray for us.

Suppose again, dear brethren, there were no conversions in our midst, would not you pray? And since there are a great many conversions, should that be a reason for leaving off? Shall we worship God the less because he gives us more? Instead of one prayer which would go up were there no conversions, there should be ten now that he continues to work salvation among us.

Suppose we were divided, and had many schisms, and jealousies, and bickerings, would not the faithful ones pray in bitterness of spirit? Will you not pray since there are no divisions, and much Christian love? Surely, I say again, you will not treat God the worse because he treats you the better. That were foolish indeed.

Suppose we were surrounded to-day with hosts of persecutors, and that error everywhere crept into our midst and did us damage, would you not pray, you who love the Lord? And now that we live in days of peace, and error, though it prowls around, is kept out of our fold, will you not commune with the Lord all the more? I will say yet a third time, shall we pray the less because God gives the more? Oh, no, but the better he is to us the more let us adore and magnify his name.

Just now we need to pray, for some are growing cold, and turning to their old sins. We need to pray, for we are doing much for Christ. Every agency is in full work. We want a *great* blessing upon *great* efforts. We have had such results from prayer as might make a man's ears to tingle who should hear of them for the first time: our history as a church has not been second even to apostolic history itself: we have seen God's arm made bare in the eyes of all the people, and to the ends of the earth the testimony of this pulpit has gone forth, and thousands have found the Saviour,—all in answer to many prayers. Pray, then, without ceasing. O church in the Tabernacle, hold fast that thou hast, that no man take thy crown. Oh, continue to be a praying church that we together, when we shall stand before the judgment-seat of Christ, pastor and people, may not be accused of being prayerless, nor of being slack in the work of the Lord. I earnestly hope all this will tend to make to-morrow's day of prayer more earnest and intense; but yet more do I pray that at all times all of us may be fervent, frequent, instant, and constant in prayer; praying in the Holy Ghost, in the name of Jesus.

10
HOW TO CONVERSE WITH GOD

"Then call thou, and I will answer: or let me speak, and answer thou me."—Job 13:22

"An obedient heart is needful if there is to be any happy converse between God and the soul."

~

JOB might well have been driven frantic by his miserable comforters; it is wonderful that he did not express himself far more bitterly than he did. Surely Satan found better instruments for his work in those three ungenerous friends than in the marauding Sabeans, or the pitiless whirlwind. They assailed Job remorselessly, and seemed to have no more bowels of compassion than so many flint stones. No wonder that he said to them many things which otherwise he would never have thought of uttering, and a few which I dare say he afterwards regretted. Possibly the expression of our text is one of those passages of too forcible speech. The tormented patriarch did what none but a man of the highest integrity could have done so intensely as he did; he made his appeal from the false judgment of man to the bar of God, and begged to be forthwith summoned before the tribunal of the Judge of all, for he was sure that God would justify him. "Though he slay me, yet will I trust in him: but I will maintain mine own ways before him. He also shall be my salvation: for an hypocrite shall not come before him." He was ready to appear at the judgment scat of God, there to be tried as to his sincerity and uprightness. He says, "Only do not two things unto me: then will I not hide myself from thee. Withdraw thine hand far from me: and let not thy dread make me afraid." He offers in the words of our text to come before the righteous Judge in any way which he might appoint—either he will be the defendant and God shall be the plaintiff in the suit— "Call thou and I will answer," or else he will take up the part of the plaintiff and the Lord shall show cause and reason for his dealings towards him, or convict him of falsehood in his pleas,—"Let me speak, and answer thou me." He feels so sure he has not been a hypocritie that he will answer to the All-seeing there and then without fear of the result.

Now, brethren, we are far from condemning Job's language, but we would be quite as far from imitating it. Considering the circumstances in which Job was placed, considering the hideous libels which were brought against him, considering how he must have been stung when accused so wrongfully at such a time, we do not wonder that he thus spoke. Yet it may be that he spoke unadvisedly with his lips; at any rate it is not for us to employ his language in the same sense, or in any measure to enter upon self-justification before God. On the contrary, let our prayer be, "Enter not into judgment with thy servant: for in thy sight shall no man living be justified." How shall man be just with God? How can we challenge his judgment before whom the heavens are not pure, and who charged his angels with folly? Unless, indeed, it be in a gospel sense, when, covered with the righteousness of Christ, we are made bold by faith to cry "Who shall lay anything to the charge of God's elect? It is God that justifieth, who is he that condemneth? it is Christ that died, yea rather, that hath risen again, who is even at the right hand of God, who also maketh intercession for us."

I am going to use the words of Job in a different sense from that in which he employed them, and shall apply them to the sweet communion which we have with our Father, God. We cannot use them in reference to our appearance before his judgment seat to be tried; but they are exactly suitable when we speak of those blessed approaches to the mercy seat when we draw near to God to be enriched and sanctified by sacred communion. The text brings out a thought which I wish to convey to you—"Call thou, and I will answer: or let me speak, and answer thou me." May the Holy Spirit bless our meditation.

The three points this morning will be, *two methods of secret converse*—"call thou, and I will answer: or let me speak, and answer thou me;" secondly, *the method of combining the two*, and here we shall try to show how the two modes of converse should be united in our communion with God; and thirdly, we shall show *how these two modes of fellowship are realized to the full in the person of our Lord Jesus Christ*, who is our answer to God, and God's answer to us.

I. First, then, here are TWO METHODS OF SACRED CONVERSE BETWEEN GOD AND THE SOUL: sometimes the Lord calls to us and we reply, and at other times we speak to God and he graciously deigns to answer us. A missionary some years ago, returning from Southern Africa, gave a description of the work which had been accomplished there, through the preaching of the gospel, and among other things he pictured a little incident of which he had been an eye-witness. He said that one morning he saw a converted African chieftain sitting under a palm tree with his Bible open before him. Every now and then he cast his eyes on his book and read a passage, and then he paused and looked up a little while, and his lips were seen to be in motion. Thus he continued alternately to look down on the Scriptures and to turn his eyes upward towards heaven. The missionary passed by without disturbing the good man, but a little while after he mentioned to him what he had seen, and asked him why it was that sometimes he read, and sometimes he looked up? The African replied,—"I look down to the book, and God speaks to me, and then I look up in prayer, and speak to the Lord, and in this way we keep up a holy talk with each other." I would set this picture before you, as being the mirror and pattern of intercourse with heaven,—the heart hearkening to the voice of God, and then replying in prayer and praise.

We will begin with the first method of communion. *Sometimes it is well in our converse with God that we should wait till our heavenly Father has spoken—* "Call thou, and I will answer." In this way the Lord communed with his servant Abraham. If you refer to those sacred interviews with which the patriarch was honoured, you will find that the record begins—"The

Lord spake unto Abraham and said." After a paragraph or two you hear Abraham speaking to the Lord, and then comes the Lord's reply, and another word from the patriarch; but the conversation generally began with the Lord himself. So was it with Moses. While he kept his flock in the wilderness he saw a bush which burned and was not consumed, and he turned aside to gaze upon it, and then the Lord spake to him out of the bush. The Lord called first, and Moses answered. Notably was this the case in the instance of the holy child Samuel. While he lay asleep the Lord said to him, "Samuel, Samuel," and he said, "Here am I," and yet a second and a third time the voice of God commenced a sacred intercourse. No doubt the Lord had heard the voice of the child in prayer at other times, but upon this notable occasion the Lord first called Samuel, and Samuel answered "Speak Lord, for thy servant heareth." So was it with Elijah. There was a still small voice, and the Lord said to the prophet, "What doest thou here, Elijah?" Then Elias replied, "I have been very jealous for the Lord God of Hosts, for they have thrown down thine altars, and slain thy prophets with the sword." To which complaint his great Master gave a comfortable answer. Now, as it was with these saints of old so has it been with us: the Lord our God has spoken to us by his Spirit, and our spiritual ears have listened to his words, and thus our intercourse with heaven has commenced. If the Lord wills to have the first word in the holy conversation which he intends to hold with his servants, God forbid that any speech of ours should interpose. Who would not be silent to hear Jehovah speak?

How does God speak to us then, and how does

he expect us to answer?

He speaks to us in the written word. This "more sure word of testimony, whereunto ye do well if ye take heed, as unto a light that shineth in a dark place." He speaks to us also in the ministry of his word, when things new and old which are in Holy Scripture are brought forth by his chosen servants, and are applied with power to our hearts by the Holy Spirit.

The Lord is not dumb in the midst of his family, though, alas, some of his children appear to be dull of hearing. Though the Urim and Thummim are no longer to be seen upon the breasts of mortal men, yet the oracle is not silent. O that we were always ready to hear the loving voice of the Lord.

The Lord's voice has many tones, all equally divine. Sometimes he uses the voice of *awakening*, and then we should give earnest heed. We are dead and he quickens us. We are sluggish and need to be bestirred, and the Lord, therefore, cries aloud to us, "Awake thou that sleepest." We are slow to draw near to him, and therefore lovingly he says, "Seek ye my face." What a mercy it is if our heart at once answers, "Thy face, Lord, will I seek." When he arouses us to duty there is true communion in our hearts if we at once reply "Here am I, send me." Our inmost souls should reply to the Lord's call as the echo answers to the voice. I fear me it is sometimes far otherwise, and then our loving Lord has his patience tried. Remember how he says "Behold I stand at the door and knock:" he knocks because he finds that door closed which should have been wide open. Alas, even his knocks are for a while in vain, for we are stretched upon the bed of ease and make idle excuses for remaining there—"I have put off my coat, how can I put it on? I have washed my feet, how can I defile them?" Let us no longer treat him in this ungenerous manner lest he take it amiss and leave us, for if he go away from us we shall seek him but find him not, we shall call him but he will give us no answer. If we will not arise at his call it may be he will leave us to slumber like sluggards till our poverty come as one that travelleth, and our want as an armed man. If our Beloved cries, "Rise up my love, my fair one, and come away," let us not linger for an instant. If he cries "Awake, awake, put on thy strength, O Zion," let us arise in the power of his call and shake ourselves from the dust. At the first sound of heaven's bugle in the morning, let us quit the bed of carnal ease and go forth to meet our Lord and King. Herein is communion, the Lord draws us and we run after him, he arouses us and we wake to serve him, he restores our soul and our hearts praise him.

Frequently the voice of God is for our *instruction*. All Scripture is written for that purpose, and our business is to listen to its teachings with open ear and willing heart. Well did the Psalmist say "I will hear what God the Lord will speak, for he will speak peace unto his people." God's own command of mercy is, "Incline your ear and come unto me, hear and your soul shall live." This is the very Gospel of God to the unsaved ones, and it is an equally important message to those who have through grace believed, for they also need to receive of his words. "Man shall not live by bread alone, but by every word which proceedeth out of the mouth of God shall men live." Hence one of the saints cried out, "Thy words were found and I did eat them;" and another said, "How sweet are thy words unto my taste, yea sweeter than honey to my mouth." God's word is the soul's manna and the soul's water of life. How greatly we ought to prize each word of divine teaching. But, dear brethren, do you not think that many are very neglectful of God's instructive voice? In the Bible we have precious doctrines, precious promises, precious precepts, and above all a precious Christ, and if a man would really live upon these choice things, he might rejoice with joy unspeakable and full of glory. But how often is the Bible left unread! And so God is not heard. He calls and we give no heed. As for the preaching of the Word when the Holy Spirit is in it, it is the "power of God unto salvation," and the Lord is pleased by the foolishness of preaching to save them that believe; but all believers do not hear the voice of the Lord by his ministers as they should. There is much carping criticism, much coldness of heart, much glorying in man, and a great want of teachableness of spirit, and thus the word is shut out of our hearts. The Lord would fain teach us by his servants, but our ears are dull of hearing. Is it any wonder that those professors cannot pray who are for ever grumbling that they cannot hear? God will be deaf to us if we are deaf to him. If we will not be taught we shall not be heard. Let us not be as the adder which is deaf to the charmer's voice. Let us be willing, yea, eager to learn. Did not our Lord Jesus say, "take my yoke upon you and learn of me"? And is there not a rich reward for so doing in his sweet assurance, "ye shall find rest unto your souls"? Search the Scriptures that no word from the Lord may be inadvertently slighted by you; hear the Word attentively and ponder it in your heart, and daily make this your prayer, "What I know not, teach thou me." "Open thou mine eyes, that I may behold wondrous things out of thy law." Let us strive against prejudice, and never let us dream that we are so wise that we need learn no more. Jesus Christ would have us be teachable as little children and ready to receive with meekness the engrafted word which is able to save our souls. You will have a blessed fellowship with your Lord if you will sit at his feet and receive his words. O for his own effectual teaching. Call thou, O Lord, and I will answer.

The Lord also speaks to his servants with the voice of *command*. Those who trust Christ must also obey him. In the day when we become the Lord's children we come under obligations to obey. Does he not himself say, "If I be a father, where is mine honour?" Dear friends, we must never have a heavy ear towards the precepts. I know some who drink in the promises as Gideon's fleece did the dew, but as for the commands, they refuse them as a man turns from wormwood. But the child of God can say, "Oh, how I love thy law, it is my meditation all the day: I will delight myself in thy commandments which I have loved." The will of God is very sweet to his children; they long to have their own wills perfectly conformed to it. True Christians are not pickers and choosers of God's word; the part which tells them how they should live in the power of the Spirit of God is as sweet to them as the other portion which tells them how they are saved by virtue of the redeeming sacrifice of Jesus Christ. Dear brethren, if we shut our ears to what Jesus tells us, we shall never have power in prayer, nor shall we enjoy intimate communion with the Well-beloved. "If ye keep my commandments, ye shall abide in my love," saith he, "even as I have kept my Father's commandments, and abide in his love." If you will not hear God, you cannot expect him to hear you, and if you will not do what he bids you, neither can you expect him to give you what you seek at his hands. An obedient heart is needful if there is to be any happy converse between God and the soul.

The Lord sometimes speaks to his servants in the tone of *rebuke*, and let us never be among those who harden their necks against him. It is not a pleasant thing to be told of our faults, but it is a most profitable thing. Brethren, when you have erred, if you are on good terms with God, he will gently chide you: his voice will sound in your conscience, "My child, was this right? my child, was this as it ought to be? Is this becoming in one redeemed with precious blood?" When you open the Bible, many a text will like a mirror show you yourself, and the spots upon your face, and conscience looking thereon will say, "Do not so, my son, this is not as thy Lord would have it." "Surely it is meet to be said unto God, I have borne chastisement, I will not offend any more: That which I see not teach thou me: if I have done iniquity, I will do no more." If we do not listen to God's rebuking voice in his word, he will probably speak in harsher tones by some afflicting providence. Perhaps he will hide from us the light of his countenance and deny as the consolations of the Spirit. Before this is the case, it will be wise to turn our hearts unto the Lord, or if it has already come to that, let us say, "Show me wherefore thou contendest with me. Make me to know my faults, my Father, and help me to purge myself from them." Brethren, be ye not as the horse, or as the mule, but pray to be made tender in spirit. Be this your prayer:

"Quick as the apple of an eye,
　　Oh, God, my conscience make,
Awake, my soul, when sin is nigh,
　　And keep it still awake.

"Oh may the least omission pain
　　My well instructed soul;
And drive me to the blood again,
　　Which makes the wounded whole!"

Let us hear Nathan as kindly when he rebukes us as when he brings a promise, for in both cases the prophet speaks his Master's own sure word. Let us thank the Lord for chiding us, and zealously set about destroying the idols against which his anger is stirred. It is due to the Lord, and it is the wisest course for ourselves.

But blessed be his name, the Lord will not always chide, neither will he keep his anger for ever. Very frequently the Lord speaks to us in *consolatory* language. How full the Bible is of comforts, how truly has God carried out his own precept to the prophet.—"Comfort ye, comfort ye my people, saith your God." What more, indeed, could God have said than he has said for the consolation of his own beloved? Be not slow to hear when God is swift to cheer you. Alas, our unbelief sometimes turns a deaf ear even to the sweetest note of Jehovah's love. We cannot think that all things will work together for our good; we cannot believe that the Providence which looks so evil can really be a blessing in disguise. Blind unbelief is sure to err, and it errs principally in stopping its ear against those dulcet tones of everlasting lovingkindness which ought to make our hearts leap within us for joy. Beloved, be ye not hard to comfort, but when God calls be ready to answer him, and say, "I believe thee, Lord, and rejoice in thy word, and therefore my soul shall put away her mourning, and gird herself with delight." This is the way to keep up fellowship with God, to hear his consolations and to be grateful for them.

And last of all upon this point, God speaks to his people sometimes in the tones which *invite to innermost communion*. I cannot tell you how they sound, your ear must itself have heard them to know what they are. Sometimes he calls his beloved one to come away to the top of Amana, to ascend above the world and all its cares, and to come to the mount of transfiguration. "There," saith he, "will I show thee my loves." There the Lord seems to lay bare his heart to his child, and to tell him all the heights and depths of love unsearchable, and let him understand his eternal union with Christ, and the safety that comes of it, and the mystical covenant with all its treasures; "for the secret of the Lord is with them that fear him, and he will show them his covenant." It is a sad thing when the Lord calls us into the secret chamber, where none may approach but men greatly beloved, and we are not prepared to enter. That innermost heart-to-heart communion is not given to him who is unclean. God said even to Moses, "Put off thy shoes from off thy feet, for the place whereon thou standest is holy ground." There is no enjoying that extraordinary nearness to God with which he sometimes favours his choice ones, unless the feet have been washed in the brazen laver, and the hands have been cleansed in innocence. "Blessed are the pure in heart, for they shall see God." He that is of clean hands and a pure heart, he shall dwell on high; and only he, for God will not draw inconsistent professors and those who are dallying with sin into close contact with himself. "Be ye clean that bear the vessels of the Lord," and especially be ye clean who hope to stand in his holy place and to behold his face, for that face is only to be beheld in righteousness.

Brethren, it is clear that the voice of God speaks to us in different tones, and our business, as his children, is to answer at once when he speaks to us. This is one form of holy fellowship.

The second and equally common form is that *we speak to God and he graciously replies to us.*

How should we speak to the Most High? I answer, first, we ought constantly to speak to him in the tone of *adoration.* We do not, I fear, adore and reverently magnify God one hundredth part as much as we should. The general frame of a Christian should be such that whenever his mind is taken off from the necessary thoughts of his calling, he should at once stand before the throne blessing the Lord, if not in words, yet in heart. I was watching the lilies the other day as they stood upon their tall stalks with flowers so fair and beautiful; they cannot sing, but they seemed to me to be offering continual hymns to God by their very existence. They had lifted themselves as near to heaven as they could, indeed they would not commence to flower till they had risen as far from the earth as their nature would permit, and then they just stood still in their beauty and showed to all around what God can do, and as they poured out their sweet perfume in silence they said by their example, "Bless ye the Lord as we also do by pouring out our very souls in sweetness." Now, you may not be able to preach, and it would not be possible to be always singing, especially in some company; but your life, your heart, your whole being should be one perpetual discourse of the lovingkindness of the Lord, and your heart, even if the Lord be silent, should carry on fellowship by adoring his blessed name.

Coupled with adoration, the Lord should always hear the voice of our *gratitude*. One of our brethren in prayer last Monday night commenced somewhat in this fashion. He said, "Lord, thou dost so continuously bless us that we feel as if we could begin to praise thee now and never leave off any more. We are half ashamed to ask for anything more, because thou dost always give so promptly, and so bountifully." In this spirit let us live. Let us be grateful unto him and bless his name, and come into his presence with thanksgiving! The whole life of the Christian man should be a psalm, of which the contents should be summed up in this sentence, "Bless the Lord, O my soul, and all that is within me bless his holy name." Now, adoration and thanksgiving, if rendered to God with a sincere heart through Jesus Christ, will be acceptable to God, and we shall receive an answer of peace from him, so that we shall realize the second half of the text. "I will speak, and answer thou me."

But, my brethren, it would not suffice for us to come before God with adoration only, for we must remember what we are. Great is he and therefore to be adored, but sinful are we, and therefore when we come to him there must always be *confession* of sin upon our lips. I never expect, until I get to heaven, to be able to cease confessing sin every day and every time I stand before God. When I wander away from God I may have some idea of being holy, but when I draw near to him I always feel as Job when he said, "I have heard of thee by the hearing of the ear, but now mine eye seeth thee; therefore I abhor myself in dust and ashes." If you would have the Lord hear, be sure you speak to him in humble notes. You have rebelled against him, you are a sinner by nature, and though forgiven and accepted, and therefore freed from dread of wrath, you can never forget that you *were* a rebel, and if it had not been for sovereign grace you would have been so still; therefore speak with lowliness and humility before the Lord if you would receive an answer.

Beloved friends, we should also speak to God with the voice of *petition*, and this we can never cease to do, for we are always full of wants. "Give us this day our daily bread" must be our prayer as long as we are in the land where daily needs require daily supplies. We shall always need to make request for temporals and for spirituals, for ourselves and for others too. The work of intercessory prayer must never be allowed to cease. Speak ye to the Lord, ye that have his ear; speak for us his servants who are his ambassadors to men, speak for the church also, plead for rebellious sinners, and ask that unnumbered blessings may be given from above.

We should also speak to him sometimes in the language of *resolution*. If the poor prodigal was right in saying, "I will arise and go to my father," so are Christians right in saying, "Therefore will I call upon him as long as I live," or in saying, "Long as I live I will bless the Lord." Sometimes when a duty is set before you very plainly which you had for a while forgotten, it is very sweet to say unto the Lord, "Lord, thy servant will rejoice to do this, only help thou me."

Register the secret vow before the Lord, and honourably fulfil it.

We should often use the language of *intimate communion*. "What language is that?" say you; and again I answer, "I cannot tell you." There are times when we say to the blessed Bridegroom of our souls love words which the uncircumcised ear must not hear. Why, even the little that is unveiled before the world in the Book of Solomon's Song has made many a man cavil, for the carnal mind cannot understand such spiritual secrets. You know how the church cries out concerning her Lord: "Let him kiss me with the kisses of his month, for his love is better than wine." There are many love passages and love words between sanctified souls and their dear Lord and Master, which it were not lawful for a man to utter in a mixed assembly, it were like the casting of pearls before swine, or reading one's love-letters in the public streets. Oh, ye chosen, speak ye to your Lord. Keep nothing from him. He has said, "If it were not so, I would have told you." He has told you all that he has seen with the Father, tell him everything that is in your heart, and when you speak with sacred child-like confidence, telling him everything, you will find him answering you with familiar love, and sweet will be the fellowship thus created.

Thus I have shewn you that there are two forms of the believer's intercourse with God.

II. Let us now consider THE METHOD OF THE COMBINATION OF THE TWO. With regard to this subject, I would say that *they must be united*. Brethren, we sometimes go to prayer, and we want God to hear us; but we have not heard what God has to say. This is wrong. Suppose a person neglects the hearing of the word, but is very fond of prayer, I feel certain that his prayer will soon become flat, stale, and unprofitable, because no conversation can be very lively which is all on one side. The man speaks, but he does not let God speak, and therefore he will soon find it hard to maintain the converse. If you are earnest in regular prayer, but do not as regularly read or hear the Scriptures, your soul gives out without taking in, and is very apt to run dry. Not only thoughts and desires will flag, but even the expressions will become monotonous. If you consider how it is that your prayer appears to lack vivacity and freshness, the probable reason is that you are trying to maintain a maimed fellowship. When conversation is all one side, do you wonder that it flags? If I have a friend at my house to-night, and we wish to have fellowship with each other, I must not do all the talking, but I must wait for him to answer me, or to suggest new topics, as he may please; and if he be wiser than I am, there is the more reason why I should play second in the conversation, and leave its guidance very much to him.

It is such a condescension on God's part to speak with us that we ought eagerly to hear what he has to say. Let him never have to complain that we turned away our ear from him. At the same time we must not be silent ourselves; for to read the Scriptures, and to hear sermons, and never to pray, would not bring fellowship with God. That would be a lame conversation. Remember how Abraham spoke with God again and again, though he felt himself to be but dust and ashes; how Moses pleaded; how David sat before the Lord and then spake with his tongue: above all, remember how Jesus talked with his Father as well as hearkened to the voice from Heaven. Let both forms of converse unite, and all will be well.

Again, it will be well sometimes to *vary the order*. Dear Mr. Müller, who is a man living near to God, whose every word is like a pearl, said the other day, "Sometimes when I go into my closet to pray, I find I cannot pray as I would. What do I then? Why, since I cannot speak to the Lord, I beg the Lord to speak to me, and therefore I open the Scriptures and read my portion; and then I find the Lord gives me matter for prayer." Is not this a suggestion of much weight? Does it not commend itself to your spiritual judgment? Have you not observed that when somebody calls to see you, you may not be in a fit condition to start a profitable conversation; but if your friend will lead, your mind takes fire, and you have no difficulty in following him. Frequently it will be best to ask the Lord to lead the sacred converse, or wait awhile till he does so. It is a blessed thing to wait at the posts of his doors, expecting a word of love from his throne. It is generally best in communion with God to begin with hearing his voice, because it is due to his sacred majesty that we should first hear what he has to say to us; and it will especially be best for us to do so when we feel out of order for communion. If the flesh in its weakness hampers the spirit, then let the Bible reading come before the praying, that the soul may be awakened thereby. Still, there are times when it will be better to speak to our heavenly Father at once. For instance, if a child has done wrong, it is very wise of him to run straight away to his father, before his father has said anything to him, and say, "Father I have sinned." The prodigal had the first word, and so should our penitence seek for speedy audience, and pour itself out like water before the Lord. Sometimes too, when our heart is very full of thankfulness, we should allow praise to burst forth at once. When we have received a great favour we ought not to wait till the giver of it speaks to us, but the moment we see him we should at once acknowledge our indebtedness. When the heart is full of either prayer or praise, and the presence of Jesus is felt, by the power of the Holy Spirit, we begin addressing the Lord with all our hearts. The Lord *has* spoken, and it is for us to reply at once.

On the other hand, when for wise reasons our Lord is silent unto us, it is well to take with us words and come unto him. If you have read your Bible, and have felt no visit from the Holy Spirit, or if you have heard a sermon and found no dew from the Lord attending it, then turn at once to prayer. Tell the Lord your condition, and entreat him to reveal himself unto you. Pray first and read afterwards, and you will find that your speaking with God will be replied to by his speaking to you through the Word. Take the two methods—common-sense and your own experience will guide you, and let sometimes one come first and sometimes the other.

But *let there be a reality about both*. Mockery in this matter is deadly sin. Do not let God's word be before you as a mass of letterpress, but let the book speak to your soul. Some people read the Bible through in a set time, and in great haste, and they might just as well never look at it at all. Can a man understand a country by merely tearing through it at a railway pace? If he desires to know the character of the soil, and the condition of the people, he walks leisurely through the land and examines with care. God's word needs digging, or its treasures will lie hidden. We must put our ear down to the heart of Scripture and hear its living throbs. Scripture often whispers rather than thunders, and the ear must be duly trained to comprehend its language. Resolve emphatically, "I WILL HEAR what God the Lord shall speak." Let God speak to you, and in order that he may do so, pause and meditate, and do not proceed till you grasp the meanings of the verses as far as the Spirit enables you. If you do not understand some passages read them again and again, and remember it is good to read even those parts of Scripture which you do not understand, even as it is good for a child to hear his father's voice whether he understands all his father has to say or not. At any rate, faith finds exercise in knowing that God never speaks in vain, even though he be not understood. Hear the word till you do understand it. While you are listening the sense will gradually break in upon your soul, but mind that you listen with opened ear and willing heart. When you speak to God do not let it be a dead form, for that is an insult to the Most High. If the heart be absent, it is as wicked to say a prayer as to be prayerless. If one should obtain an audience of Her Majesty and then should read a petition in which he took no interest, which was in fact a mere set of words, it would be an insult of the worst kind. Beware lest you thus insult the Majesty of heaven!

III. The last thought is only meant to be dropped before you for you to enlarge upon it at your leisure,—THE BLESSED REALIZATION OF THESE TWO FORMS OF COMMUNION IN THE PERSON OF CHRIST.— "Call thou, and I will answer." Infinite majesty of God, call thou upon me and ask thou for all thou canst ask, and I bless thee that I have an answer for thee. Ask thy poor servant for all thou canst demand of him and he will gladly reply. Brethren do you ask in wonder—How can we answer him? The answer is clear—By bringing Jesus to remembrance. Our Lord Jesus Christ is man's complete answer to God. Divine justice demands death as the penalty of sin:—Behold the Son of God taken down from the cross because he was surely dead, wrapped in the cerements of the grave and laid in Joseph's tomb. God's justice demands suffering, demands that the sinner be abandoned of God. See yonder cross and hear the cry, "My God, my God, why hast thou forsaken me?" Great God, thou hast in Jesus all the suffering thy justice can ask, even to death itself. God's holiness righteously demands a life of obedience: man cannot be right before God unless he renders perfect obedience to the law. Behold our answer, we bring a perfect Saviour's active and passive obedience and lay it down at Jehovah's feet—what can he ask for more? He requires a perfect heart, and an unblemished person, and he cannot accept less than a perfect manhood. We bring the Father his Only Begotten, the Son of man, our brother; and here is our answer: there is the perfect man, the unfallen head of the race. Oh, never try to reply to God with any other answer than this. Whatever he asks of thee, bring him thy Saviour; he cannot ask more. Thou bringest before him that which fully contents him, for he himself has said, "This is my beloved Son, in whom I am well pleased." Let thine answer then to the justice of God be Christ.

But I said that Christ fulfilled the other purpose. He is God's answer to us. What have you to ask of

God this morning? Are you so far away from him that you enquire, "How can I be saved?" No answer comes out of the excellent glory except Christ on the cross, that is God's answer: believe in him and live. By those wounds, by that bloody sweat, by that sacrificial death, you must be saved; look you there! Do you say unto the Lord, "I have trusted Christ, but am I secure of salvation?" No answer comes but Christ risen from the dead to die no more. Death hath no more dominion over him, and he hath said, "Because I live ye shall live also." The risen Christ is the Lord's assurance of our safety for eternity. Do you ask the Lord, "How much dost thou love me?" Thou hast asked a large question, but there is a large answer for thee. He gives his Son, behold what manner of love is here! Do you enquire, "Lord, what wilt thou give me?" His Son is the answer to that question also. Behold these lines written on his bleeding person, "He that spared not his own Son, but delivered him up for us all, how shall he not with him also freely give us all things?" Would you know more? Do you say, "What sign showest thou that all these things are so?" He gives thee Christ in heaven. Yea, if thou askest, "Lord, what shall thy servant be when thou hast completed thy work of grace upon me?" he points you to Jesus in the glory, for you shall be like him. If you ask what is to be your destiny in the future, he shows you Christ coming a second time without a sin-offering unto salvation. Dear friend, thou canst ask nothing of thy God, but what he gives thee at once a reply in Jesus. Oh what blessed talk is that when the Christian's heart says *Jesus*, and the Christian's God says *Jesus*, and how sweet it is when we come to Jesus and rest in him, and God is in Jesus and makes him his rest for ever. Thus do believers and their God rest together in the same beloved One. May the Lord add his blessing to our meditation, and make this kind of communion common among us for Jesus' sake. Amen.

ABOUT THE AUTHOR

Charles Haddon Spurgeon, known as "The Prince of Preachers", was a famous Reformed Baptist preacher born in Essex, England in 1834. A full-time preacher by the age of 17, Spurgeon preached an estimated 3,600 sermons by the time of his death in 1892. Spurgeon frequently preached to audiences larger than 10,000, while his printed sermons reached tens of thousands more each week.

Spurgeon authored almost 50 volumes including the classic works *All of Grace, Morning & Evening, The Power of Prayer in a Believer's Life, Lectures to My Students,* and *The Treasury of David: A Commentary on the Psalms.* More than a century after his death, Spurgeon's devotional writings continue to touch hearts around the world. Once when asked the secret of his success, Spurgeon replied, "My people pray for me."

MINISTRIES WE LOVE

Cross-Points Books loves organizations committed to building Christ's church by proclaiming the gospel, resourcing leaders, and training workers for the harvest. Here are some of our favorite ministries:

9Marks — Building Healthy Churches (www.9marks.org)

Desiring God — Helping people understand and embrace the truth that God is most glorified in us when we are most satisfied in him. (www.desiringgod.org)

Matthias Media — An evangelical publisher of gospel-centered resources. (www.matthiasmedia.com)

Leadership Resources — A global ministry training pastors in 30+ countries to preach expository sermons, train other expositors, and foster movements of God's Word. (www.leadershipresources.org)

The Gospel Coalition — Encouraging and educating Christian leaders by advocating gospel-centered principles and practices that glorify the Savior and do good to those for whom he shed his life's blood. (www.thegospelcoalition.org)

Unlocking the Bible — Delivering the gospel through modern media. The teaching ministry of Colin S. Smith. (www.unlockingthebible.org)

CONNECT WITH CROSS-POINTS

For news on upcoming releases and deals on resources
promoting sound doctrine and godly devotion,
visit Cross-Points.org or follow us on social media.